MOTO GUZZI

MOTO GUZZI

Mick Walker

OSPREY
AUTOMOTIVE

Published in Great Britain in 1993 by Osprey,
an imprint of Reed Consumer Books Limited,
Michelin House, 81 Fulham Road, London
SW3 6RB and Auckland, Singapore.

Reprinted autumn 1997

ISBN 1 85532 720 1

Managing Editor Shaun Barrington
Editor Julia North
Page design Paul Kime/Ward Peacock

Printed in Hong Kong

Front cover
*Moto Guzzi 1100 Sport, 1996. The
machine had a conventional two valves
per cylinder pushrod engine, unlike the
fuel injected, four-valve per cylinder 'high
cam' Daytona. Though fuel injection is
now available on the Sport. The idea
was to produce a less expensive sports
bike, using the same frame and many of
the same styling cues as the Daytona.
Some people actually prefer the looks of
the cheaper bike. (Roland Brown)*

Back cover
*The most famous of all Moto Guzzi's big
twins, the Falcone, first introduced in
1950. Carlo Perelli described the Falcone
as 'the most romantic 500cc in the
world.' Romance is not often the word
for a motorcycle, but here it feels
absolutely right*

Half-title page
*The Dr John Wittner-inspired Daytona
with belt-driven ohc. This is the 1994
Team Raceco race bike at Brands Hatch*

Title page
*The magnificent 1000 Daytona engine
has breathed new life into an ageing
design*

Right
*Carlo guzzi's last design, the 175 Lodola
ohc single. Of special interest are the
inclined cylinder and heel and toe
gearchange with indicator*

*Illustrations from Mick Walker's
collection; with grateful thanks to Gary
Clarke, Brian Fox, Terry Howe, Kel Edge
and Roland Brown for additional
photographs*

For a catalogue of all books published by Osprey Automotive
please write to:
**The Marketing Department, Reed Consumer Books,
1st Floor, Michelin House, 81 Fulham Road, London SW3 6RB**

Introduction

In Italy, there is one motorcycle marque that stands above all others when it comes to history and tradition: Moto Guzzi.

Today Guzzi is seen very much as a traditionalist, but this was not always so. From its inception shortly after the Great War, its initial efforts remain shining examples of vision and achievement – and this would continue until the end of the 1950s, some four decades later. From its Mandello del Lario factory came a constant stream of mould-breaking designs which were to achieve glory on both road and track.

From the start, Moto Guzzi realized the importance of racing as an effective means of publicity, and were active in this branch of the sport until their final withdrawal at the end of the 1957 season.

During this period, Guzzi had an engineering team which could match the best anywhere in the motorcycle world. These technicians will forever be remembered, not only for the string of World Championships and TT victories but their amazing versatility in racing design. In addition to a whole series of successful singles they were also responsible for various other configurations, including V-twin, across-the-frames, in-line 4, and V8 engines.

Guzzi also built its own wind tunnel facilities to test and develop streamlining for their machines, which contributed enormously to their racing and record breaking feats.

On the production side, following the Second World War, Guzzi reinforced its position as the largest of all Italy's bike builders with a range which not only included the ever-popular horizontal four-stroke singles but a new series of small capacity two-strokes (many with rotary valve induction), and an interesting motorcycle-cum-scooter called the Galletto.

Other popular post-war singles, both four-strokes, were the Lodola and Stornello; but then, in the late 1960s, the once great factory struck hard times. It was eventually saved by the Argentinian business tycoon Alejandro de Tomaso, who set about rebuilding both profits and model range.

Not only did de Tomaso save Guzzi, he also cashed in on the 90° V-twin range which had begun in the mid-1960s with the first V7, established several joint venture 'badge engineering' exercises with Benelli and, perhaps his biggest achievement, masterminded an entirely new family of middleweight V-twins which today extends from 350 through to 750cc.

Right
The California is Guzzi's longest running v-twin model. It is available with cast or wire wheels; carburettors or fuel injection; in LAPD (shown) or touring trim. Latest version has 1100 motor

Contents

Founding Fathers

On either side of Lake Como stands high mountainous terrain. The town of Lecco is at the southernmost tip of the lake, and to the traveller arriving from the urban and industrial flatlands of Milan, the shock to the system is breathtaking. The road into Lecco leads over a long bridge into the streets of the town, many of them still wearing the cobbles of antiquity.

A casual visitor might never notice the sign to the left which takes the initiated to Mandello del Lario, the home of Moto Guzzi, along a series of tree-lined streets at the edge of the lake. As the town is left behind, the road ahead can be seen to cling perilously to the base of the steep mountainside, ensuring that the highway itself twists and turns around the contours of the water. Quite often, it passes through the man-made galleries which have been erected to protect traffic from the dangers of landslides and rockfalls. This lasts for around six or seven miles when, all of a sudden, around yet another bend, the cliff-face retreats, a road sign leaps forward proclaiming 'Mandello del Lario' and the visitor finds himself within a sizeable township, housing not only the population but also Italy's most famous motorcycle factory.

Moto Guzzi's story is as romantic as its setting, dating back to the closing years of World War One and the idealistic dreams of a young airman. The youthful Carlo Guzzi was summoned to serve his country at the outbreak of war, initially in the army, but as the struggle wore on he transferred to the fledgling air corps. It was this which was to prove the spur to the start of a motorcycling legend.

Guzzi, now a mechanic and driver, came into contact with two flying officers, Giorgio Parodi and Giovanni Ravelli, both young men of means from wealthy and influential families. Parodi's family were an old established dynasty of ship owners from the port of Genoa, while Ravelli, whose home was Brescia, a large town situated between Milan and Verona, was already well known in sporting motorcycle circles, having competed with distinction in a number of pre-war racing events.

The trio soon became friends with a shared interest in motorcycling, and planned a business association when the war came to an end. Guzzi would design, Parodi organize the finance, and Ravelli ride the machine to glory on the race circuit. Sadly, Ravelli was not to live long enough to see his own particular dreams come true. A few short days after the end of hostilities in the autumn of 1918, he lost his life in a flying accident. The winged-eagle emblem carried by almost all of the company's motorcycles, even to this day, is dedicated to his memory.

Despite this sad setback, Parodi, as good as his word, came up with the

Co-founder of the Moto Guzzi marque and its chief designer for almost four decades, Carlo Guzzi 1889-1964

The company's famous eagle emblem has its origins in the Italian Air Corps of the First World War

necessary financial backing to enable a prototype to be constructed. The money for the project, which the surviving partners had decided to continue, was provided by Parodi's father, Emanuele. The now-famous letter in which he granted approval is kept is kept in the Guzzi museum within the factory at Mandello, and in translation tells the story: 'So the answer you should give your companions is that on the whole I am in favour of the idea, that 1500 or 2000 Liras for the first experiment are at your disposal provided this figure is absolutely not exceeded, but that I reserve the right to personally examine the design before giving my final support for seriously launching the product, because in the fortunate event that I like the design I am ready to go much further with no limitation on the figure.'

It is important to realize from the outset exactly what type of men Carlo Guzzi and Giorgio Parodi were. Although of different backgrounds – Guzzi had been brought up within a relatively poor family in the urban sprawl of Milan - they both shared a common bond in that, above all, they wanted the project to succeed, even if it meant accepting the other's arguments. This, together with the stabilizing influence brought to bear by Parodi Senior, was to see the partnership through the demanding early days.

However, in terms of their individual personalities, they were totally at odds. Carlo Guzzi was a reserved, quiet man who was entirely ensconced in his experiments and theories, and once convinced of the rightness of a design principle he would never be tempted to exceed what he considered to be the 'safe' way financially. In other words, he was not a man to take

Mandello del Lario, the home of the Guzzi factory since 1920. This photograph was taken in 1954

any unnecessary financial risks. Parodi, on the other hand, was flamboyant and impulsive. It was a combination of both their respective natures which was to provide just the right ingredients for success. Without a doubt, had Carlo Guzzi been left totally to his own devices, his brilliant designs would never have reached the public's attention. Conversely, had Giorgio Parodi taken control of the company itself, it could well have gone up like a shooting star, only to crash spectacularly soon afterwards!

Work on the first prototype machine was not completed until well into 1920. When shown to Parodi Senior, everyone was happy; not only did he give his seal of approval, but he also commented on how much he was impressed by the finished product – and so it was all systems go (although that is not how they would have put it in 1920). Parodi Senior was as good as his word, and duly proffered additional funds.

Called simply the GP (Guzzi and Parodi), the prototype was for its day

a glamorous device full of real technical innovation. It was dominated by its engine, which showed a marked tendency toward aeronautical design practice with its four parallel valves which were operated by a single overhead camshaft driven by shaft and bevel gears. There was also a dual ignition system and twin sparking plugs fired by a single German Bosch magneto. But perhaps even more interesting was its adoption of the layout which was to characterize the marque for half a century - a single cylinder laid horizontally with unit construction of engine and transmission. A prominent characteristic of the design which was also to endure for a long period was the 'bacon slicer' shape of the external flywheel. Another feature was Guzzi's adoption of the oversquare engine dimensions of 88 x 82mm bore and stroke.

Almost all of this was unheard of in its day. Not only was unit construction - with geared primary drive as well - virtually unknown, but so was a horizontal cylinder assembly and a bore which was larger than the stroke.

The frame was a sturdy affair with twin front downtubes which passed either side of the cylinder head. Completing the picture came a pair of girder front forks, with dual springs placed centrally just forward of the steering column, square-section mudguards, a sprung single saddle, and a single brake which operated on the rear wheel. The front wheel carried a massive gear (like a sprocket) which drove the speedometer. The three-speed gearbox was operated by a large hand lever mounted on the right of the flat, box-like fuel tank.

The first word of the new machine (now renamed Moto Guzzi) to reach the outside world came in the 15 December 1920 issue of *Moto-ciclismo* magazine. The name change had come about because Giorgio Parodi had not wanted the 'GP' to be taken as his initials and had suggested that it should be called Moto Guzzi, meaning simply Guzzi Motorcycle.

There had been a number of changes in the Guzzi Motorcycle which was offered for sale to the public. The original design had been very much an expression of Carlo Guzzi's idealized concept of how a motorcycle should be in engineering terms. This was not quite the same thing as when viewed from a production viewpoint and consequently, for economic reasons if nothing else, the motorcycle offered for sale to the public was substantially redesigned. With the uninspiring name of Normale (meaning standard), it reverted to more conventional practices in some departments. The most obvious alteration was the replacement of the overhead cams and four valves by a pair of opposed valves with the inlet in the head, controlled by a rod and rocker arm, and a side-valve exhaust. This arrangement, known as inlet over exhaust (ioe) was very much in line with practice of contemporary manufacturers.

Above

Another feature of Moto Guzzi is its comprehensive museum. In the foreground is a V-8 racer, together with a spare engine unit

Right

Police and army contracts have played a vital role in Guzzi's history. This montage shows the involvement down through the years including Italian and Dutch military; and police forces from Africa, Asia, America and Europe

MOTO GUZZI

La Moto Guzzi ha da sempre fornito moto per usi militari o
attrezzate per polizia a molti paesi del Mondo.
Ultimamente è stata prescelta dal Ministero della Difesa
Olandese per una importantissima fornitura di veicoli in versione
Militare con delle specifiche caratteristiche "NATO" riconosciute
fra le più sofisticate. Prima di essere accettati i veicoli sono stati
sottoposti all'esame strutturale di tutti i materiali impiegati ed al
collaudo della funzionalità nelle più gravose ed imprevedibili
condizioni di utilizzazione, con una serie di test estremamente
seri e complessi, che richiedono l'evidenza dalle più alte
tecnologie impiegate.
Tutte le Moto Guzzi per servizi speciali sono costruite con quelle
particolari specifiche, siano esse destinate a Servizi Municipali
che ad impieghi Militari.
È la garanzia Moto Guzzi da oltre 65 anni.

GBM S.p.A. 22054 Mandello del Lario (CO) - Via E.V. Parodi, 57 - Tel. (0341) 709111 - Fax (0341) 709220 - Tlx 380095 GUZZI I

Big Singles

Between 1940 and 1943 Guzzi built over 8000 of their famous 500cc flat singles for use by the Italian military. These served with distinction on every front from the arid North African deserts to the vast Russian steppes in the eastern sector. Over a quarter of these machines were the Trialce three-wheeler; based on the civilian Motocarro.

Even after the Second World War, Guzzi was to provide the majority of machines for both the military and police – a tradition that continues to this very day.

However, probably the most famous of all Guzzi's big singles was the Falcone, which first appeared in 1950 and which was to become in later years one of the all-time classics of the Italian motorcycle industry. Just why the Falcone was able to carve such a special niche among the real enthusiasts might seem a little hard to justify on paper, as it was in truth only an up-date on an old theme and the replacement for the long-running GTW model. But, ride a Falcone and the answer becomes much clearer. Summed up perfectly from a 1960s Carlo Perelli road test quote: 'The Moto Guzzi establishment on the shores of Lake Como continues to produce what must surely be the most romantic 500cc single in the world.' In describing the Falcone at a time when it had been re-introduced by

Left
The first production Moto Guzzi, the Tipo Normale. Built between 1921 and 1924, this 498cc single was capable of just under 50mph

Above right
First offered in 1931, the Sport 15 remained in production until 1939 and proved an excellent machine in service

Right
Sport 15 engine pumped out 13.2 bhp offering its rider a 62 mph top speed on the highway

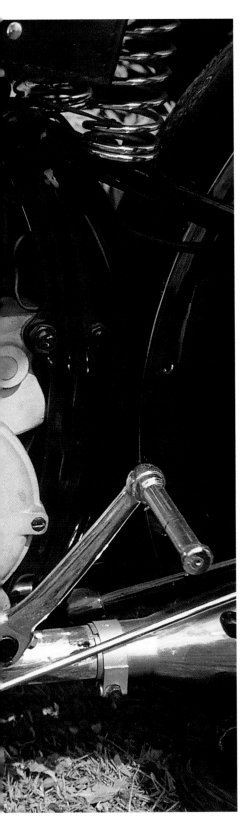

popular demand in 1963, Perelli went on to explain exactly what he meant by the word 'romantic'. This, he said, was a vintage-looking machine which nostalgically retained features which had completely disappeared from other designs over the previous decade and more.

The bike Perelli was talking about was precisely the same Falcone as that which, in 1950, entered the world as a direct descendant of the roadster V model introduced in 1934 in the GTV, GTW and GTC, culminating in the GTCL (Gran Turismo Corsa Leggera, or, quite literally, grand touring light racer!). This, in turn, became the Condor of 1938, although the road version was really a 'racer with lights'. After the war, the Condor became the faster Dondolino, and then the faster still Gambalunga. Meanwhile, the 'cooking' GTV was given an alloy cylinder head and barrel, becoming the Astore in the process. And after adopting the Condor-type gear cluster and other bottom-end refinements, the GTW became the Falcone!

Interestingly, from the cylinder head-barrel down, the Falcone and

Above
Another uniform Guzzi layout on its big singles was the handlebar control layout; best described as vintage, it lasted through to the early 1960s

Left
Traditional big single Guzzi features include 'Bacon slicer' outside flywheel, Dell'Orto carburettor and horizontal cylinder

Condor engines (and hence the Dondolino) were virtually identical in all but the minor details and material. The crankcases, for instance, were absolutely indistinguishable except for the engine number and their weight – the Condor's were in electron-magnesium alloy, while the Falcone's were plain aluminium alloy. The cylinder head was similar with regard to the port size and shape, valve sizes and other aspects, but the racers had exposed valve springs whereas the Falcone had all its oily bits decently covered.

What all this meant was that a Falcone could be made to go. In standard trim Guzzi claimed 135kmh (85mph), but with Dondolino cam, piston and carb, a souped-up Falcone could go at Dondolino-type speeds – 170kmh (106mph). Here, in fact, lies one of the reasons why the Falcone was to gain such esteem – much as BSA's famed Gold Star did in Britain.

This tuneability also enabled Moto Guzzi themselves to gain valuable publicity, scoring some notable successes in many of the long-distance road events in the early 1950s. In such classics as the Nord-Sud, Milano-Taranto and Giro d'Italia, these factory-entered Falcones looked at the time to be nothing more than well-prepared standard production roadsters; but inside, where it counted, they were 100 per cent Dondolino.

When launched in 1950, the Falcone was only offered in civilian guise to one specification. This followed almost the same state of tune as the GTW – same compression, same maximum revs – but with 1bhp more, and the alloy head and barrel, enclosed rocker gear and SS 29A racing carb, which is what made all the difference. The primary transmission was by helical gear, with 44- and 78-tooth pinions, giving a ratio of 1.77:1; although the clutch itself was unaltered. The first-gear ratio was 2.29:1, second 1.713:1, third 1.317:1, and fourth direct 1:1. Final drive was by a slim ⅝ x ¼ in chain with 16- and 36-tooth sprockets, giving a 2.25:1 reduction.

In the appearance stakes, the Falcone definitely had a clear edge over its predecessor, with a new lower frame, more sporting 17.5-litre tank, a pillion pad in place of the metal mudguard-top carrier, almost flat narrow bars and no legshields. The oil tank, however, stayed in the same place and retained the same capacity.

More powerful electrics were another improvement. The dynamo was now a 60 watt Marelli DN36 unit, geared at 1.33:1 and with Marelli's IR39C regulator, plus a battery which had increased in capacity to 13.5 amp/hr. On the first model, the magneto had manual advance and retard, but this was replaced in 1952 by an automatic unit.

For the 1954 season, the place of the now discontinued Astore model

Viewed from another angle this 1930s Sport 15 displays its ioe (inlet over exhaust) engine, heel and toe gearchange, oil tank and large Marelli horn

was taken by a detuned version of the Falcone. It was then that both versions were given the official titles of Sport and Turismo. The latter was pure plodder, with a top whack of only 120kmh (75mph). Other differences were smaller valves, a 5.5:1 compression ratio and Dell'Orto MD 27F carb, resulting in a power output of 18.9bhp at 5300rpm.

Both the gearbox and primary drive remained the same, but the final drive ratio was altered to suit the Turismo's unspectacular role. This was achieved by giving the rear wheel sprocket three more teeth, dropping the ratio to 2.437:1.

Like the GTV and Astore, the Falcone Turismo carried 3.50 x 19in tyres front and rear, did not offer its owner the 'luxury' of a speedometer, and lacked the chromed knee sections on the tank which were now black. However, the remainder of the machine, except for minor parts like the stand and headlamp shell, which were also black, was finished, like the Sport, in bright Italian racing red. Wider handlebars with a rearward pull-back were fitted, as were the much bemoaned (though appreciated for protection) pressed-tin legshields.

And this is how both models remained until the Falcone civilian line

The 500 GTV was built between 1934 and 1946 and in original form featured ohv and almost 19bhp. This 1940 model has the rare Testa Velox cylinder head

Testa Velox cylinder head conversion not only gave fully enclosed valve gear protection, but also a useful benefit in extra performance

was rationalized and 're-launched' by popular demand in 1963. When this happened, strangely enough it was not the Sport, but the Turismo (complete with legshields) which was on offer. About the only difference in specification was a new silencer without the traditional fish-tail end.

This is the type that I rode on one of my first visits to Italy in the early 1970s. Immediately after I saw the Falcone I realized exactly what Carlo Perelli had meant in his 1963 comment about 'romantic'. There is an undeniable old-world charm that centres on the terrific pulling power provided by a big slow-revving, almost lazy engine. Even in its 1960s form it retained a magneto and separate dynamo to attend to the lighting requirements, an exhaust valve lifter, a carburettor devoid of air filtration, and even the 1920s-type Guzzi spring frame with a pair of 'springs-in-a-box' under the engine. If one thing alone (besides the engine) told me I was riding a piece of yesteryear, it was the inverted clutch and front brake levers, surely the last such fitted to any motorcycle in the world. Yet, to ride it was to revive old pleasures as one pottered along quiet country lanes at near walking pace in top gear or, still in top, successfully tackled a climb or hairpin bends with the engine turning over so slowly that it

Left

A Falcone Turismo, eager for a blast even on a cold, misty autumn morning. Its blend of moderate performance, low revving engine and safe handling provide motorcycling at a leisurely gait – unmatched by more modern machines

Right

Making its debut in 1950, the famous Falcone model was eventually offered in both Turismo and Sport form as this factory brochure shows

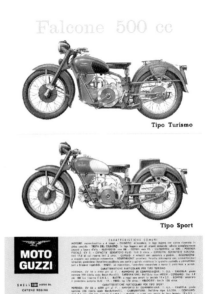

Falcone 500 cc

Tipo Turismo

Tipo Sport

was almost possible to count the individual strokes!

Thanks to the valve lifter, I found the engine always willing to start. Tick-over was so slow that you could hear the carburettor intake hiss as it drew in each separate lung-full of fresh air. I can only imagine that it was this charm, and the fact that, by then, the Falcone was seen very much as an 'old man's machine', that led the factory to choose the Turismo instead of the Sport format.

Performance proved to be a genuine 75mph – and this was attainable under almost any conditions - even with those massively proportioned legshields in place. Although they added nothing to the sporting line of the machine, they did provide truly superb protection against the elements for the rider's legs and feet.

I found fuel consumption never dropped below 60pg, even when the Guzzi was ridden flat out for miles on end. When taking it easy, this improved to over 80-mpg and must say something for the benefits of such a low state of tune and excellent torque figures.

Officially, the factory records show that the last 'civilian' Falcone of this type was produced in 1967, although for many years afterwards dealers throughout Italy offered ex-police or military models to the public at the end of their service life. So ended what could reasonably have been expected to be the Falcone's span of natural life.

But this was not to be. In response to continued and clamorous pressure from Guzzi die-hards who demanded one of the big flat singles and nothing else (in a similar way to the mid-1980s BMW flat-twin buffs

wanting boxers and not the newer K series), Guzzi finally relented and came up with the Falcone Nuovo.

First details of the new Falcone, originally intended only for military/police use, appeared in the press during November 1969, and it finally became available to the public in 1971 at a price of 612,000 lire in Italy (it is interesting to note that the 1963 price of the re-launched 'old' Falcone was 423,000). But although the engine retained the Falcone's original dimensions, almost everything else was different. This was no mere rehash of the old bike, but a complete redesign of both the engine and running gear.

Externally, the most obvious changes to the flat single were the large, finned 3-litre capacity wet sump – so the oil tank was no more - electric start (there were 12 volt electrics), square-slide Dell'Orto VHB 29A carb, and a far more compact and tidy line to the full unit-construction engine. The cylinder barrel, in aluminium like the head, had a steel liner which allowed it to be rebored – unlike contemporary Guzzis which were using chrome-plate straight on to the alloy. Guzzi's press handout claimed that the power output was 30bhp at 5000rpm, but in truth it was 26.2 at 4800. Fortunately, Guzzi did not pander to fashion by offering a fifth gear, which could only have been a sales gimmick on such a slow-revving, torquey engine.

Above

Classic Falcone finish of bright Italian red paint work with gold pinstriping; it is set off by a mass of bright alloy and sparkling chrome

Above right

Another feature of the vast majority of big singles from the famous Mandello del Lario factory is the lovely fishtail silencer; manufactured in the same village by the Lafranconi concern

Right

Besides its popular 500 single, Guzzi also offered the 250 Airone.
This is the Sport version with its higher compression engine, thicker valve springs and SS1 25A Dell'Orto racing carburettor

The new power unit was slotted into a totally new double-cradle tubular-steel frame, with fully enclosed front and rear suspension, and full-width 200mm Grimeca drum brakes (twin leading-shoe at the front). At 185kg (407lb) dry, the Nuovo was some 15kg heavier than the old Falcone, but in its favour were its improved handling and braking - and not least, the fitting of decent electrics at last. The factory offered a few touring goodies for the Falcone Nuovo, including colour-matched panniers and a chrome-plated front crash-bar.

Unlike previous Falcones, the finish was not entirely red as the tank, panels, mudguard and chain-guard were in a sharply contrasting brilliant white, setting off the red frame, swinging arm and forks. Black was used for minor parts like the rear suspension upper shrouds, the stands (both centre and prop-stands were fitted as standard), rear light body, and headlamp shell. There were 'Falcone' decals in red with a black line above

Above
Separate float bowl with central tickler for Dell'Orto carb, separate magneto and dynamo atop crankcase, enclosed valve gear and giant external flywheel are all clearly visible in this view

Right
With the actual springing contained in boxes underneath the motor, damping was achieved via adjustable friction device shown here. Also note finned brake drum, lockable side boxes and welled alloy rims

for the side panels, and on the tank a gold Guzzi winged eagle emblem above the name 'Moto Guzzi' in dark blue between two light-blue lines. Rounding off the package, the light-blue lines were repeated along both sides of the mudguards.

Although most brochures of the period show a single Lafranconi-seamed silencer with a 'slashed' rear end, most production models were initially produced with a ridiculous twin version. From 1971 to 1974, Guzzi insisted on fitting their single with what amounted to a rather poor-looking copy of the paired pipes from one side of a four-cylinder racing machine. As it was, the effect on a soft, woolly tourer was totally wrong and out of place on what was supposed to be a practical (if somewhat staid) machine for the older enthusiast. If such a device had been fitted to something like a sporting bike for the younger rider, it might just have worked, but on the Nuovo Guzzi, no! The prototype had carried a different system, which was also to appear on some of the later models. Although still in effect a twin unit, this was more practical – if ugly – with a pair of silencers stacked one above the other like bunk beds.

In 1974, the machine received something of a mini face-lift. There were

CEV headlamp, centrally mounted kph Veglia clock with Guzzi inscribed upon its face, 'Ace'-type bars and lever-action fuel filler cap

Airone Sport at rest. In the immediate post-war years this quarter litre machine was Guzzi's best selling four-stroke model. It combined excellent fuel economy with a respectable 70 mph plus top speed

new chrome-plated mudguards and headlamp shell, and a new colour scheme with revised decals. The finish was now an attractive metallic cherry red for the tank and side panels, with the rest of the paintwork in black. The 'Falcone' decals on the side panels were in white, while a new design of 'Moto Guzzi' logo appeared for the tank. again in white, this featured a thick and thin line running all the way along each side of the tank under the words, with the winged eagle above.

More importantly, 1974 also ushered in a completely new version, the Sahara. Very much a civilian version of the military Falcone, finished in sand and black, the military theme was carried into the robust single seat and austere matt black 'stacked' double-barrel silencer. There was a one-piece console instead of the separate instruments on the Falcone Nuovo, but standard equipment included engine covers, a chrome crash-bar, and colour-matched (sand) panniers. The tank was shorter and wider than the original but still retained its 18-litre capacity. It was adorned with a simple 'Moto Guzzi' emblem in black, and the word 'Sahara' was inscribed in an Arabic style along the side panels.

In 1975, during one of my visits to the Mandello factory to collect a parts shipment in my role as British spares importer, I discussed with export manager 'Joe' Ermilini the possibility of importing the Sahara into Britain. Quite simply, this was because I felt that it would appeal to a small band of single-cylinder enthusiasts who were at the time bemoaning the non-availability of just such a motorcycle since the passing of the last of the British big singles, and then in 1974 the end of production of both the 350 Harley-Davidson (Aermacchi) and the Ducati ohc models. But this plan never got off the ground as it was vetoed by the firm then responsible for British imports of Guzzi motorcycles, Coburn & Hughes, who had no interest in single-cylinder machines. In any case, this would have only provided a new source of singles for a short period, as Guzzi themselves discontinued all versions of the Falcone at the end of 1976.

What I find fascinating is that, right to the end, it is possible to draw up a family tree of Guzzi four-stroke flat singles dating from 1921 in a continuous unbroken chain of improvements and developments. It can be carried even further. The very first Guzzi 500 single – and all later versions except some of the Works Gambalunga racers – shared common 88mm bore and 82mm stroke measurements. When the V1000 Convert automatic was announced in the mid-1970s, the first 1000cc (948cc actually) V-twin seemed as far removed from that first spindly production machine of 1921 as it was possible to get. Yet check the bore and stroke and, as you will have guessed, there they are at 88 x 82mm!

Whatever may follow in motorcycling, a record like that is hardly ever likely to be broken.

Right

Terry Howe took this picture of Swiss Peter Zurcher's 500 Guzzi single at the Isle of Man Manx Rally in 1993, a machine which is ridden by its owner on a regular basis. Note larger touring tank and non-standard hi-bars

Left

Guzzi brought out the Nuovo (new) Falcone during late 1969. Except for its engine capacity and bore and stroke dimensions it shared nothing with the old. The motor was of full unit construction, with electric starter as an option. Also new were 12 volt electrics, the frame, suspension and brakes

Above

The civilian Nuovo Falcone followed the military/police model into production during the early 1970s. Despite the major redesign, performance at 81 mph was no improvement

Lightweights

Prior to the end of the Second World War, Moto Guzzi had never sold anything under 175cc, and certainly no two-strokes. However, all this was to change over the next quarter of a century with a plethora of lightweights in a variety of engine sizes, in two- and four-stroke.

The decision to move down-market was taken for the soundest of commercial reasons. Pre-war, the motorcycle had not, for the most part, been viewed in Italy as anything other than a sporting vehicle for the die-hard enthusiast. However, with the cessation of hostilities, the four-wheel fleet almost annihilated, public transport in disarray, and fuel and raw materials at a premium, the lightweight motorcycle appeared (and was largely accepted) to be the answer to the population's need for mobility.

Some of the machines were basic in the extreme, some were expensive but unreliable, some manufacturers saw the answer in the micromotor-assisted bicycle, whilst yet more considered the scooter was the future.

But of course Guzzi, with their traditional leading position within the Italian industry, opted for another solution: a high-quality lightweight powered by an extremely efficient rotary-valve two-stroke engine. The result was the 65 Guzzino (little Guzzi).

This tiny newcomer was the work of Ing Antonio Micucci, who had

Guzzi provided Italy's best-selling immediate post-war motorcycle, the two-stroke Motoleggera 65. Its rotary valve engine provided economical transport to countless thousands in those austere times

Imported into Ireland by ex-factory Guzzi rider Stanley Woods, this immaculate 175ohc Lodola dates from the late 1950s

joined Guzzi in the winter of 1942. He was appointed Managing Designer in 1945, and the new two-stroke was his first design in this post.

The rotary-valve motor had a capacity of 64cc (42 x 46mm). Running on a low 5.5:1 compression ratio, thanks to the low octane fuel then available, the Guzzino produced a modest 2bhp at 5000rpm, giving it a top speed slightly over 30mph – a figure which could be achieved virtually regardless of load. But its real forté was its quite amazing fuel consumption – up to 200mpg!

The cylinder head and barrel were both cast in light alloy, and the barrel featured a cast-iron liner. Lubrication was provided by petrol/oil mixture at a ratio of 20:1. Carburation was taken care of by a 13mm Dell'Orto.

The transmission consisted of helical-geared primary drive, a wet multi-plate clutch and a 3-speed hand-operated gearbox, the lever of which was mounted on the offside of the 6 ½-litre fuel tank.

Few changes were introduced to the Guzzino's specification during its production run except for a horn and modified silencer tail pipe in 1948, a strengthened rear fork in 1949, and a move to a cast-iron barrel in 1953.

Left

First introduced in 1959, the larger capacity 235 featured overhead valve instead of overhead camshaft and remained in production until it was finally phased out in 1966

Below

The 1966 40cc (37 x38 mm) Trotter moped was the final design of Ing. Antonio Micucci who had joined Guzzi in the winter of 1942. Appointed Managing Designer in 1945 he had gone on to design the Guzzino 65, Cardellino and Zigolo; not to mention the innovative 250 parallel twin GP bike of the late 1940s

Besides selling in excess of 200,000 units between 1946 and 1954, the tiny machine was pressed into service by a wide range of customers, including several who even went as far as fitting a sidecar. If this was not bizarre enough, an after-market conversion kit was offered by a Bergamese concern which transformed the tiny engine into a 73cc four-stroke, complete with fully-enclosed valves, and a lubrication system made up of a gear-type feed and return pump.

The Guzzino's successor was the Cardellino. Initially the only two differences to the original model were smaller wheels (down from 26in to 20in), and a redesigned rear frame – a result of the often excess loads of passengers and goods with which owners had subjected the tiny Guzzi two-stroke to in the past.

The first real changes to the specification came in 1956, when early that year the Cardellino gained a pair of undamped telescopic forks, replacing the original blade-type which had also been a feature of the Guzzino since it entered production a decade earlier. The mudguards were also replaced by a new design which provided increased protection, and full-width alloy brake drums were fitted.

Later the same year at the Milan Show, a larger capacity variant was announced, known as the '73'. This reflected its increased capacity, achieved by adding 3mm to the bore (45mm). Other improvements saw the power output rise to 2.66bhp, and the replacement of the tank-mounted hard gearchange to a more modern foot-operated lever.

Subsequent up-dates saw a flashed-chromed alloy cylinder (1959) and a

MOTO GUZZI

trotter

By 1973 there were three distinct Stornello models; the 125, 160 and, a 125 Scrambler. This machine differed from its roadster brothers in having braced bars, chrome head lamp, competition-style front forks, sump guard, hi-level exhaust and knobbly tyres. Note revised engine outer covers compared with earlier Stornello models

further increase in capacity (83cc – 1962). Production was finally brought to a close in 1965.

In reality, it was not the Cardellino but the 98cc (50 x 50mm) Zigolo which took over the 'best selling' tab from the Guzzino. This was first seen at the Milan Spring Fair in April 1953 and for its day brought an air of sophistication to the previously lacklustre ultra-lightweight category.

Far from being simply a larger bore Guzzino, the majority of Zigolo's specification was brand new, and once again came from the design-hand of Signor Micucci.

Although still of the rotary valve-type, the engine now featured a totally horizontal cylinder, with its Dell'Orto carburettor mounted on the opposite side to the smaller unit. Running on a compression ratio of 6:1, its 4bhp output provided a top speed of 47mph.

The Zigolo employed a pressed-steel chassis, with partial enclosure. Whilst in the suspension department, the new Guzzi lightweight carried a

pair of undamped teles at the front, with the rear springing being taken care of by a rubber element in compression with friction-type damping. Yet another departure was the use of smaller diameter 19in wheels, allied to 2.50 section tyres.

Apart from the 'cooking' Lusso model, Guzzi also offered the Zigolo Sport which had its debut in 1954. Basically it was the same bike, but with a tweaked engine – with power boosted to 6.8bhp and a maximum speed of 56mph.

In 1958 came the 98 Zigolo Series II. Together with the Cardellino, the new bike was the first Italian series production model to feature an alloy cylinder without the conventional cast-iron liner. Instead, a layer of hard chrome-plating was applied directly to the alloy, employing a special electrolytic process conceived in Germany. This allowed the engine to employ reduced piston-to-bore clearances and still require less lubrication. In fact, the petrol-oil ratio was reduced from 20:1 to 50:1, resulting in not only superior performance but far less exhaust pollution. The down-side was that, should the bore become damaged, the only remedy was a new barrel – a costly move.

Badge engineering via Guzzi's marriage to the Benelli marque resulted in several machines such as the 250 TS two-stroke twin (offered between 1974 and 1982) ...

... and the 125 four-stroke 2C4T which was virtually half a 254 four cylinder 250. Its single overhead cam engine pumped out 16bhp at 10,600 rpm and a five-speed gearbox helped to keep the tiny unit on the boil

For the 1960 model year, Guzzi increased the Zigolo's engine size to 110.3cc – upping both the bore and stroke by 2cc (52x52mm). Performance, however, was no better than the 98cc Sport model. The Zigolo survived one year longer than the Cardinello, and it was 1966 before the axe fell.

Other two-stroke Guzzis from Ing Micucci were the 49cc (38.5 x 42mm) Dingo ultra-lightweight motorcycle (produced in GT, Super, MM, 3V, and Cross varieties) between 1967 and 1976; plus the Trotter commuter moped.

Into the De Tomaso era, and a totally new series of Guzzi 'strokers' made their bow, including the Chiù step-thru moped, Cross 50, 125 Turismo/Tuttoterreno, and 250 TS twin. However, these were not really Guzzis at all, but simply badge-engineered Benellis! The same applies to the water-cooled 125 Custom which made its début at the Milan Show in November 1985.

The other half of the Mandello lightweight story is taken up by three distinct four-stroke series: the Galletto, Lodola, and Stornello. The first of these to appear was the Galletto (Cockerel), best described as a motorcycle-scooter hybrid. The prototype Galletto was revealed to the public at the

Swiss Show in Geneva during March 1950, with a capacity of 150cc. But by the time production commenced later that year, engine size had been upped to 159.5cc (62 x 53mm). Soon output reached 3000 examples per month, making the hybrid a corner-stone of the factory's success in the immediate post-war period.

At the end of 1952, the engine size was again enlarged, this time to 174.4cc (65 x 53mm). Further changes came in 1954 with the capacity again made bigger, this time to 192cc (65 x 58mm).

The final redesign came seven years later in 1961, but this time it was the rest of the bike, rather than the engine, which received attention; with brand new bodywork, rear suspension and electrics (which included electric starting for the first time). When it was finally taken out of production at the end of 1966, Guzzi's 'Cockerel' was truly missed, winning as it had many admirers during its long lifespan.

Another much-loved Mandello lightweight was the Lodola, Carlo Guzzi's final design. The original Lodola, which appeared in 1956, displaced a chain-driven single overhead camshaft. Later in 1959, the capacity was increased to 235cc (68 x 64mm), the other major change being a substitution of the overhead cam valve gear with more humble pushrod operation.

Features of both versions included a cylinder inclined 45° from the vertical, full unit construction, telescopic front forks, twin shock, rear suspension, twin front down-tube frame, dry sump lubrication, 18in front and 17in rear wheels, and a front primary drive gear of most unorthodox design; being manufactured in two parts.

Besides the 175 and 235 roadster models, Guzzi built a number of works Lodola ISDT bikes in both capacities, plus a full-blown 250. All three versions of the dirt iron competed with distinction in the *Six Days* from 1959 through to the mid-Sixties, winning a clutch of gold medals along the way. But as far as the roadsters were concerned, they were very much soundly engineered touring bikes rather than out-and-out sportsters.

Finally, there was the Stornello. Built over a fifteen-year period in 125 form (and eight years as a 160), it was built down to a cost, hence its pushrod single-cylinder engine and basic specification. Nevertheless, both versions of the Stornello proved themselves robust and relatively trouble-free for countless thousands of customers both in Italy and abroad. The Stornello was also one of the few Guzzis to transcend the original management at the De Tomaso takeover.

Like the Lodola before it, the Stornello (125 only) was to be built in

The final Guzzi lightweight was the 125 BX trail bike of the 1980s. Its 124cc (52.5 x 55mm) two-stroke motor featured a lamellar valve; a custom version was also offered. This was another Benelli-inspired design

limited numbers for competition use in long distance trials. It was also the first four-stroke lightweight from the famous Mandello Del Lario factory, the last examples rolling off the production line in mid-1975.

Dirt Irons

One of Guzzi's most underrated niche markets for its long-running series of V-twins has been the on-off road motorcycle.

The first to appear were the V35/65TTs. The 'T' designation did not stand for Isle of Man Tourist Trophy, but instead the initials stood for Tutto Terreno (all-terrain). From an industry more well-versed in the

Below

Guzzi's first try at making a trail bike out of the V-twin was prototype-only V50TS, which appeared on the company's stand at the 1981 Milan Show; it never reached production

Right

Although the V50TS didn't make it beyond the prototype stage, Guzzi didn't bin the idea. Next, in 1984 came the V65TT (and its little sister the V35 TT). Both were to prove, with only a couple of potential snags, excellent at the dual on/off road task. TT stood for Tutto Terrano (all-terrain), not the Isle of Man races

Above

Guzzi even went to the trouble and expense of building a pukka racing dirt iron in the shape of the 1985 V65 TT Baja. This very special bike was clearly intended for not only the famous Baja event in Mexico, but also the Paris-Dakar and the Pharoah's rallies

Left

By 1987 the TT models had been phased out in favour of the new NTX, again available in both 350 and 650 engine sizes. The machines were largely unchanged mechanically from their predecessors. The smaller mount had a striking yellow/ white/ black livery ...

lightweight, narrow power band, marginal reliability two-stroke enduro bikes, the Guzzi blend of middleweight/heavyweight, torquey and virtually 'bullet-proof' ohv four-stroke V-twin green lanes bike went down well. Its nearest rival was not Italian, but the German BMW GS series.

These initial two models used the basic engineering from their respectively standard roadster V35/65 brothers (as with the custom variants), but cosmetically the pair of TTs were quite a departure. Topped off by a pukka Moto X-style 14-litre fuel tank, the styling exercise was surprisingly effective with generally smooth, flowing lines which continued down through the side panels and rear seat/mudguard section. The seat covering was in a fashionable red with 'TT' embossed in blue, and a nose at the front which extended up and over the rear of the tank. Components such as the switchgear and instrumentation remained unaltered. The prop-stand only was used, and a couple of sensible additions came in the form of rubber gaiters for the one-off leading axle Marzocchi forks, together with a comprehensive rubber mud-flap that extended down to protect the timing cover at the base of the front guard.

Plastic was used for the enduro style front light/number-plate support at the front mudguard. Both these were colour matched with the tank, side panels, and rear seat support.

Other features included a black (rust-prone) two-into-one-into-two exhaust, Akront alloy rims, 21in and 18in front and rear tyres, knobbly

Above

… whilst the 650 had a far more restrained red/white/black paint job. The 350 was aimed almost exclusively at the home market, whilst the bigger NTX was exported in considerable numbers. Besides an entirely new (but still black) exhaust system there was also a much wider use of black, including the entire engine and final drive assemblies

Right

For the 1990s the NTX was given a 'Paris-Dakar' look which transformed its image overnight. At the same time, the larger capacity model became a 750, with 743.9cc (80x74mm). Weighing in at 180kg, maximum speed rose to 106mph

Above and right

But even the 750 NTX was eclipsed by Guzzi's new monster trailie, the 1000 Quota. Instead of attempting to extract more power from the 750 version, the factory opted for the 1000 Le Mans type engine in an all-new chassis. The Quota's specification includes 125mph performance, alloy rims and electronic ignition. (Photograph right, Roland Brown)

tyres, pillion footrests, and a rear carrier. A notable feature was that the front and rear brakes (both 260mm drilled discs) relied on conventional operation, not the linked system found on other Guzzi V-twins.

Most owners and magazine testers were full of praise for both the 350 and 650TTs' performance on road and dirt, even if for the latter they were a touch too heavy.

From this initial attempt, Guzzi developed the idea further: first with a 750NTX (743.9cc – 80 x 74mm), and finally with a 1000 Quota (948.8cc – 88 x 78mm). The bigger bike weighed in at 210kg (460lb) and had a top speed of 125mph. Unlike earlier models, it had single shock rear suspension, a twin headlamp fairing, purpose-built frame, and a motor based on the big-bore Guzzi rather than one which originated in the same V35/75 series.

Racing

In the glamorous world of motorcycle racing, Moto Guzzi will forever be remembered for its amazing versatility in design. In addition to the famous horizontal singles, it produced machines with V-twin, across-the-frame three-cylinder, inline four-cylinder, horizontal four-cylinder, and even V-8 engines! Not content with that, the Mandello concern constructed its own wind tunnel to test and develop streamlining for its bikes, which played an important role in the successful family of racing and record-breaking machinery.

The roll of famous riders to have ridden for the Italian factory is no less impressive with men such as Ghersi, Woods, Tenni, Sandri, Foster, Cann, Barrington, Ruffo, Lorezetti, Anderson, Dale, Kavanagh, Lomas and Campbell, to name but a few.

Guzzi's first competition event came in the 1922 Milano-Napoli (Nord-Sud) long-distance race in which Aldo Finzi finished twentieth with team mate Mario Cavendini two places further back. Both riders were mounted on 498.4cc (88 x 82mm) singles.

One month after this début, Aldo Finzi's brother, Gino, gave Guzzi their first taste of glory when he won the prestigious Targa Florio – a classic race in which both cars and motorcycles took part, around the mountainous terrain of Sicily.

Thereafter, success followed success, with victories coming thick and fast in such events as the Giro d'Italia (Tour of Italy) and the Circuito del Lario, the latter being best described as the Italian equivalent of the Isle of Man TT.

A new 4-valve model appeared in 1924 and with it the marque gained its first major victory outside Italy, the German Grand Prix, staged over the famous banked Avus circuit in Berlin.

Not content to rest on its laurels, Guzzi then brought out a smaller version of its proven single with a capacity of 248.8cc (68 x 68mm). On this, Pietro Ghersi created a sensation in the Isle of Man TT that year by finishing runner-up, only to be disqualified in controversial circumstances for using a different make of spark plug to that stated on his original entry form!

After this setback, it was not until nine years later that the team were to

Top privateer Arthur Wheeler – a motorcycle dealer from Epsom, Surrey. Wheeler rode a variety of 250 and 350 Guzzi singles for a decade from 1952 until he retired in 1962. He then made a return to take part in Classic racing during the 1980s. Today, well into his seventies, he is still to be seen in action

Above

Arthur Wheeler's Reynolds-framed 350 (75x80mm) Guzzi single. The frame's most unusual feature is its massive backbone top tube which doubles as an oil tank, brakes and forks are factory Guzzi components. The bike in this form was constructed in the winter of 1961/62

Left

When Arthur Wheeler retired at the end of 1962, his Guzzi stable was used for a time by Londoner Trevor Barnes, who is seen here on his way to victory at a BMCRC (Bemsee) club event at Snetterton in September 1964

The fabulous 498.7cc (44 x 41mm) Guzzi V8 Grand Prix machine. Raced in 1956 and 1957, it was not fully developed when the factory pulled out of racing at the end of 1957. The machine shown here is being demonstrated by the former Guzzi world champion, Bill Lomas

taste success in Monas Island, when Irishman Stanley Woods won both the Lightweight (250) and Senior (500) TTs. Woods' victories were also in many ways the starting point for a sustained effort in the pre-war days, with another victory coming in the 1937 Lightweight TT, and the epic defeat of the mighty DKWs in the 1937 250cc German Grand Prix.

Remaining faithful to its horizontal single-cylinder model, Guzzi dominated the post-war class from 1947 to 1953. Then the company enlarged the engine capacity, entered the 350cc class and astounded the racing world by winning the World Championship at its first attempt.

Much of this success was due to the fact that Scot Fergus Anderson, who had first ridden Guzzis in the late 1940s, became 350cc champion in 1953 and again in 1954, before becoming director of the factory's competition department – he was back on the track again in 1956, but was tragically killed that year at the Belgian Floreffe circuit riding a 500 BMW at the age of 47.

However, Anderson had laid the foundations, all thanks to the technical expertise and the brilliant technical wizardry of Ing Carcano. Guzzi went on to even greater things not only retaining its 350cc world title in 1955, 1956 and again in 1957 – against the might of the four-cylinder Gilera and MV Agustas – but developing the world's first and only V8 Grand Prix motorcycle.

The V8 represented the very peak of design achievement in the 1950s, an era which in retrospect (and to date) was truly the golden age of post-war motorcycle racing.

Right

Another Bol d'Or shot, this time of a Guzzi competitor in the 1982 24-hour endurance event. This machine was the fastest Guzzi that year. Ridden by the team of Micheli/Gambini/Tamburini, it lost 2.5 hours in the night stemming an oil leak, but still finished 36th

Above left

At the Imola 200 race in April 1972, three works 750 Guzzis appeared. Built in just six weeks, they finished 8th, 10th and 11th, ridden by Brambrilla, Findlay and Mandracci.
The engines based on the production V-7 Sport model were tuned to give 80 bhp and were capable of over 140mph

Below far left

A Moto Guzzi Le Mans 1 (25) awaits the start of the Battle of the Twins support race at the 1985 Bol d'Or in France. Also in the frame is another Guzzi (60) a Ducati 750 F1 (94) and a Ducati Pantah (99)

Below left

A rather special 500 Guzzi horizontal single, seen at an 'Old timer' racing event at the Nürburgring, Germany. (Photograph Kel Edge)

The 498.7cc (44 x 41mm) power unit with gear-driven double overhead camshafts and water-cooling was the most advanced motorcycle engine of its time. With a wide spread of power (between 7000 and 12000rpm), it only required four gear ratios, and produced 75bhp. Before retiring from the 1957 500cc Belgian GP, one was timed at 178mph; a phenomenal speed some three-and-a-half decades ago. Raced in 1956 and 1957, it was not fully developed when Guzzi pulled out of racing at the end of 1957. Had the factory continued, most informed observers agree that it would most likely have dominated the Blue Ribband 500 Grand Prix circuit over succeeding years. Instead, the surviving machine, together with a spare engine unit, are today to be found in the famous museum housed within the Mandello plant.

Instead, Guzzi went trials-riding in the late 1950s and 1960s with machines based on its Lodola roadster model, gaining a string of gold medals in the ISDT.

It wasn't until many years later in October 1969 that the Moto Guzzi name once again graced the headlines of the press with its tarmac achievements; and when this came, it was in the record-breaking, not racing, area.

Using specially-prepared versions of its then new large capacity ohv V-twin, a team of riders blasted around Monza to take fifteen world records in the solo and sidecar classes. To enable the firm to capture the maximum number, two engine sizes were prepared: 750cc – 739.3cc (82 x 70mm) and 1000cc – 757.5cc (83 x 70mm).

Two-and-a-half years later on, 23 April 1972, three Works-prepared 750 V-twins took part in the first Imola 200 mile racer. Built in just over six weeks by a team led by Ing Tonti, they finished eighth, tenth and eleventh, ridden by Brambrilla, Findlay and Mandracci.

The engines, based on the production V-7 Sport model, were tuned to give around 80bhp, and the riders were able to rev them to 8400rpm in the gears and 8000rpm in top.

Guzzi employed a new type of Dell'Orto carburettor, and experimented with both 38mm and 40mm instruments. Also used were triple hydraulically-operated disc brakes, with British Lockheed calipers. From these, Imola bikes came a series of endurance racing bikes which took part

Above
Battle of the Twins racing, which began in the early 1980s, has become popular on both sides of the Atlantic. 1000 Guzzi rider Greg Birkett is seen here with his BOT racer at Cadwell Park in April 1991. Specification includes Carillo con-rods, Astrolite wheels, Öhlins rear shocks and braced forks

Right
One of the most successful riders in British Twins racing has been Ian Cobby, seen here wheeling his Chris Clarke-entered machine at Cadwell Park, 1991. Brief specification: Trans Kontinental clutch, Dr John 'F' cam, 2 plug heads, 41.5mm carbs and Astrolite wheels

in events such as the Barcelona 24-hours Bol d'Or and Spa 24 hours, with a fair amount of success during the mid-1970s. Privateers even continued campaigning Guzzi V-twins into the 1980s.

Finally, there have come the various models, most notable of which was the Dr John Wittner machine (effectively the prototype for the Daytona) which are to be seen in Battle of the Twins events. So, even today, over 70 years after the first Guzzi race victory, the famous eagle emblem is still to be seen on the race tracks of the world. How many other marques can boast this record?

Above
Spondon Engineering of Derby constructed this one-off prototype framed Guzzi racer in 1992. Features include 17 inch Marvic wheels, Showi (Ducati 888) front forks, floating discs, Dutch White Power rear shock and 22° steering head angle

Left
Another Cadwell Park shot, this time of Tim Wild and his truly immaculate Le Mans 1 based BOTT racer, summer 1992. Note deep sump and huge Dell'Orto pumper carbs

Raceco had a new bike – still a Daytona – and a new rider, Richard Defango; the pairing seen here in action at Cadwell Park, April 1994. The team is a joint venture between Raceco boss Amedeo Castellani and British importers Three Cross

Above
Unidentified rider hanging well out from his Guzzi V-twin in a German Battle of the Twins race, 1993. (Photograph, Kel Edge)

Right
The 1993 British BEARS (British, European and American Racing) championship was won by a Ducati 888; however this race-kitted Daytona came home second, ridden by Torquil Ross-Martin. Race preparation was looked after by Amedeo Castellani of Raceco, London

V7

Few motorcycle engines have had a stranger beginning than the large capacity Moto Guzzi V-twin. Its origins were owed entirely to the Italian military authorities' extraordinary 3 x 3 go-anywhere tractor. The 3 x 3 must surely rank as one of the most bizarre-looking vehicles of all time. However, it used a 90° pushrod V-twin of 754cc – which was to spawn the classic range of Guzzi V-twin motorcycles.

The original 3 x 3 project began back in the late 1950s when the Italian Defence Ministry in Rome conceived a requirement for a go-anywhere, lightweight tractor to operate under almost any condition, over any terrain, including deep sand or snow. The result being a vehicle which was able to achieve some truly amazing feats – including the ability to climb almost vertical surfaces!

And it was Italy's military (and civil) authorities which were also to play a vital role in the V-twin power unit (based on that used in the 3 x 3), with their need in the early 1960s for a suitable replacement for its ageing Guzzi flat single Falcone models, used in considerable numbers throughout Italy for both military and police work.

The original prototype of what was ultimately to emerge as the V7 motorcycle was started in 1964. Early the following year, the first pre-production models were being presented for governmental approval. Even

Powerful, fast, smooth, and quiet the Moto Guzzi V7 twin is the machine
Puissante, rapide, souple et silencieuse, la V7 c'est la deux-cylindre du
Kraftvoll, Schnell, Geräuschlos, die V7 ist ein Zweizylinder für echte

One of the first 700 V-7 production models seen on the company's 1967 brochure, with the background of Lake Como. The full brochure caption reads 'Powerful, fast, smooth and quiet, the Moto Guzzi V-7 twin is the machine for the most discriminating enthusiast and for unlimited touring'

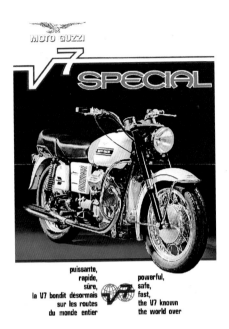

at this early stage, the Guzzi management realized that here was a machine destined for success in the wider field of everyday riding. The first civilian prototype appeared in public in December 1965 at the thirty-ninth international Milan Show. Hailed immediately by journalists and show-goers alike as the star exhibit, its commercial future was assured.

However, unlike Guzzi's legendary post-war racers – which had been designed by the same brain which had created the V7 – the new V-twin had been designed by Ing Giulio Cesare Carcano with a definite emphasis on its original military and police role, rather than as a sportster. Not only did this show up in its simplicity and ease of maintenance, but also in its surprisingly agricultural appearance – especially when compared with the more technically sophisticated exotica of the Superbike era, into which its long life was to take it.

The V7 name was taken from the engine's transverse 90° V-twin layout, and its original capacity of 703.717cc. The ohv power unit had over-square dimensions with bore and stroke of 80 x 70mm, and on a compression ratio of 9:1 it gave 40bhp at a leisurely (by later standards) 5800rpm.

The engine layout gave the big Guzzi its own trademark, and its simplicity and initial soft state of tune endowed it with a long and usually trouble-free life. It was these characteristics which were to prove the design's strongest and most appealing assets down through the years.

The V7's concept was aimed at the most simple solution to an engineering problem but there were one or two features which seemed at

A brochure showing the 1970 V-7 Special, the European version of the American Ambassador model. First introduced in 1969 this had seen the capacity grow to 757.486cc, achieved by increasing the bore to 83mm while the stroke was unaltered at 70mm

First model to sport a capacity of 850 (actually 844.057 cc) was the GT (Eldorado in the States). This made its bow at the Milan Show in November 1971, and was offered between 1972 and 1974

direct odds with this line of thought. Most notable was the use of chrome-plated cylinder bores. Although theoretically technically superior (offering closer finning tolerances and longer life in ideal conditions), in practice it could prove expensive if the bore became worn or was damaged through misuse (running short of oil for example). Whereas a cast iron liner could be rebored several times, the only solution to a worn or damaged barrel was a new barrel and piston assembly.

The one-piece steel crankshaft used bolt-up big-end eyes running on thin wall split-shell big-end bearings. Like the main bearings, these were made from Al-TIN alloy and were available in various oversizes. The original thickness of standard big-end bearings was from 1.534mm to 1.543mm, and undersize half bearings were available in 0.254mm, 0.508mm, 0.762mm and 1.016mm. Mains were originally from 37.995mm - 37.959mm in diameter for the front mainshaft (flywheel) bearing, and 53.970mm - 53.931mm for the rear (timing) bearing. Undersizes were made in 0.2mm, 0.4mm, 0.6mm, and 0.8mm thicknesses. Both the crankpin area and the main bearing surfaces were constructed so that if very slight seizing marks were detected these could be eliminated using fine carborundum; but if the surfaces were deeply scored or worn over, regrinding had to take place before the next bearing size could be used. After a regrind, it was necessary to restore the shoulder relief radiuses, 1.5mm for the crankpin and 3mm for the mainshaft at the flywheel end.

Like the one-piece crankcase and cylinder barrels, the cylinder heads were constructed in light alloy, and they were each retained by four long and two short studs passing through the cylinders and screwing into the crankcases. Oil tightness was ensured by a paper cylinder base gasket and six cylinder head bolt 'O' rings per cylinder. The head gasket was a thick car type sandwich.

Each exhaust port was threaded in the alloy to receive a matching screwed nut and proved to be continually problemlatic until completely superseded in the mid-1970s by a totally new method. On the V-7 model the exhaust ring tended to come loose and if not attended to quickly would ruin the alloy thread in the head. The only way of preventing this was to wire lock the ring. But, obviously, once the damage had been done it was too late.

The inlet had separate stubs. These were bolted in place with a heat resistant gasket and three large Allen screws, ready to receive the pair of Dell'Orto SSI 29 carbs originally fitted.

Easy access to the valve gear on each side was provided by a large alloy rocker cover and held in place with eight Allen screws and a one-piece gasket. Underneath this cover, a cast iron one-piece detachable support held each pair of rockers in place. The tappets were of the simple adjuster screw and lock-nut type. The valves themselves were inclined at 70°, and a 34.6mm exhaust and 38.6mm inlet were used. These were fitted with single coil springs seated on special cast-iron inserts.

The camshaft was centrally located between the cylinders, and the base of each pushrod located on a tappet which ran on the appropriate camshaft lobe. The front of the camshaft was connected to the large upper timing gear, part of a matched train of three helical cut steel gears for the timing and oil pump drive, housed in the timing chest at the front of the engine. The other end of the camshaft incorporated a worm gear to drive the Marelli car-type distributor located at the base of the right-hand cylinder.

Engine lubrication was looked after by the 3-litre (5 ½ pints) heavily finned, detachable wet sump which acted as an oil tank, and the gear-type oil pump housed in the base of the timing chest on the left-hand side and driven by the lowest of the three gears which connected to the central crankshaft timing pinion. The pump itself consisted of a pair of gears, with the serviceable width of between 15.983mm and 15.994mm, housed in an alloy pump body.

Pressure in the system was maintained at a constant level by the oil pressure release valve fitted inside the crankcase on the section which supported the sump. This valve was pre-set at the factory to a delivery pressure in the circuit of 2.5 to 3kg/cm2 (35.6-42.7lb/sq in). If the pressure rose above the prescribed rating, the valve would open through a pipe situated on top of the engine, into a metal breather box and then by hose into the atmosphere. An oil pressure switch fitted externally on the top of the crankcase activated an oil pressure warning light which was situated on the instrument console.

The oil pump drew a steady supply from the sump and, after passing it through a wire gauze strainer, delivered the oil through ducts in the crankcase. These directly supplied the oil under pressure to the main bearings, the camshaft housings and the crankshaft, through which it passed to lubricate the big-end bearings. Oil passing out around the big-ends was flung out to lubricate the cylinder walls and the remainder of the engine by splash. The cylinder heads received their own, separate supply through external oil feed pipes.

The big Guzzi's transmission system owed more to four wheels than two. Bolted to the rear of the crankshaft was a large diameter flywheel which also formed the housing for the dry clutch. This consisted of two friction and two plain plates, and eight springs. The clutch assembly was retained inside the flywheel by the electric starter ring gear. Passing through the centre of the clutch shaft was a single long clutch pushrod, which then passed through the input shaft of the gearbox to exit behind the clutch operating lever on the back of the gearbox.

The gearbox shell was bolted onto the rear of the crankcase. It had four

Right
Slim, low and aggressive, the 1972 V-7 Sport marked a new chapter in the evolution of the large capacity Guzzi V-twin. Designed by Ing Lino Tonti, the sportster was everything the original V-7 was not

Below right
As well as using an alternator for the first time (enabling a much lower frame to be used), the other significant engine change was the new capacity of 748.8cc. Higher compression, four-ring, 9.8:1 pistons were used, while a more sporting cam profile, paired coil valve springs and larger 30mm Dell'Orto carbs completed the specification

speeds (five speeds didn't appear until the 1972 model year) and was of the constant mesh, frontal engagement type. The mainshaft was driven by the driving gear on the clutch shaft. All four gears were fixed to the mainshaft – a one-piece assembly. The layshaft was provided with four separate engagement gears, two sliding sleeves and also carried the speedometer drive gear.

The gears were selected directly by the gear lever, this controlled the selector shaft which had a toothed sector in mesh with a gear on the selector drum. The drum carried a series of grooves in which the selector mechanism ran, so that its position, and the position of the gears which it selected on the layshaft, was governed by the rotation of the selector. In the drum were five holes, one for each gear, plus neutral and a spring-loaded pawl ensured that it was positively located in each of the positions in turn as the gear lever was operated. A little-known fact is that the pawl was drilled and worked additionally as a gearbox breather. In addition the gearbox was provided with a neutral indicator switch.

Rear drive was courtesy of Cardan shaft and bevel gears, a feature which was to prove one of the most important in the design's success. The drive was taken from the rear of the gearbox via splines on the end of the gearbox layshaft which connected to a universal joint running in a 28 x 58 x 16mm ball race housed in the end of the swinging arm. The exposed section between the swinging arm and the rear of the gearbox was protected by a rubber gaiter to accommodate the suspension movement. Inside the swinging arm, the universal joint mated up with drive shaft which ran in two 25 x 52 x 16.25mm ball races, one at each end. At the rear, this was splined to the bevel drive pinion inside the rear drive box, an aluminium casting filled with EP90 oil to lubricate the drive. The crown wheel was meshed directly with the pinion, and mated up with the rear wheel through an internally-toothed sleeve in the rear hub. The rear wheel could be removed without the need to disturb the drive simply by removing the wheel spindle and spacer which kept the wheel centred and in mesh.

For its day, the V-7's electrical system was sophisticated (certainly by Italian standards!) with a powerful 12 volt system with a 300 watt Marelli DN62N generator located on top of the crankcase between the cylinders in front of the oil breather box and driven from the crankshaft by two pulleys and a rubber belt. The belt ran down in front of the timing cover, and a large alloy outer casing between the two cylinders down to the base of the timing cover was fitted over the belt pulleys and the front of the generator to protect them from road dirt and the elements.

The generator was retained in position by a split metal band and was covered from either side by separate steel pressings. The generator charged a massive 32 amp hour battery, needed mainly because no kick-start was fitted and, very unusual for the time, the machine relied entirely on its electric starter. This was a Marelli MT40H motor, a four-pole design with an output of 0.7hp and rotating clockwise. It was mounted on the rear nearside of the crankcase engaging with the flywheel ring gear via a Marelli IE13DA solenoid fitted directly below the starter motor.

Ignition was again by Marelli, with an SI23A distributor housing a single set of points and condenser. This was driven by a worm on the camshaft and provided sparks via a single Marelli or Bosch ignition coil.

The remainder of the V7 was much more in line with other Italian models of the period with CEV lighting and switchgear, a sturdy duplex frame, enclosed telescopic front forks (with 35mm stanchions), full width 220mm brake hubs (a 2LS at the front), alloy wheel rims, adjustable rear dampers, Veglia instruments and a large 20-litre (4 ½ gallons) fuel tank, with chrome-plated knee recesses.

With a maximum speed of just over 100mph, the V7 was decidedly better at touring that as a sports bike; and in any case it certainly didn't look very fast with its heavyweight appearance.

Although first displayed at the end of 1965, the first civilian versions didn't hit the dealers' showrooms until the spring of 1967. The following year, 1968, saw the 700cc V-7 continue, but now with a new starter motor and the carbs changed to square slide Dell'Orto VHBs – although retaining the 29mm choke size. 1969 saw a bigger change when an enlarged version called the V-7 Special made it bow.

The capacity had grown to 757.486cc, achieved by increasing the bore to 83mm while the stroke was unaltered at 70mm. A new type of piston was used – although there were still four rings – the oil scraper was moved up to join the other three (originally the oil scraper had been below the gudgeon pin), and the skirt was relieved to give an almost semi-slipper appearance. There were still 'A', 'B' and 'C'-type pistons with micro measurements as before, but now with a prefix of 83mm.

The rest of the engine assembly displayed only small changes – although considerably assisting performance. The valves were increased in size to 36mm exhaust, 41mm inlet. They also gained smaller internal valve springs fitted inside the main coils. The clutch springs were changed too, for a slightly stronger type. Engine oil pressure was increased: 3.8 to 4.2kg/cm2 (54 to 60lb/sq in). Power was now up to 45bhp at 6000rpm. Although the gearbox remained a four-speeder with identical ratios, the bevel drive ratios were changed to 8.35 giving a new higher gearing of 4.375:1. Finally, helped by a drop in kerb weight from 243kg (530lb) to 228kg (502lb), maximum speed increased to 115mph.

In North America the V-7 Special was marketed as the Ambassador. Both versions were manufactured between 1969 and 1971, before production ceased at the end of 1971 to make way for two machines which would both – although of differing concepts – play a vital role in the future development of the big Guzzi V-twin line.

These newcomers were the 850GT and V-7 Sport. The GT was a very much larger capacity version of the original V-7 concept, but with an even larger engine of 844.06cc. The increase was achieved not by increasing the 83mm bore, but by lengthening the stroke to 78mm. The 9.2:1 comp pistons had three rings instead of four, and power output rose to 51bhp at 6000rpm.

There was also an American customized model released at the same time, the GT California. This was very much a no-compromise custom cruiser with standard equipment – a large screen, laid-back high and wide western bars, a black and white buddy saddle, rear carrier, 1950s style Harley-type panniers (but in fibreglass), plus additional chrome-plate – including the crash-bars front and rear, and the deeply-valanced mudguards. Mechanically, and in their basic running gear, both the 850GT and California remained largely as before. This was was not the case with the other half of the 1971 Show duo, the V-7 Sport which, as I stated in my book *Moto Guzzi Twins* was 'a real sports motorcycle'.

To many enthusiasts the V-7 Sport is a true classic and today rivals the 850 Le Mans I, the most collectable of all Guzzi's many V-Twin models. This 1972 model is an American-market model with a different colour scheme to the European version

Previously, as with the new GT models, the Guzzi V-twins had been a decidedly touring package. But with the slim, low and aggressive V-7 Sport, a new era had begun for the Mandello company. It was this model which outlined the path which all the large capacity Guzzi twins over the next twenty-five years would follow.

Ing Carcano retired in 1967, and the man who succeeded him, Lino Tonti, was to be responsible for transforming a previously overweight and, some would say, ugly machine into a real sportster. Tonti had joined Guzzi following a string of appointments with names such as Aermacchi, Bianchi, and the small concern which manufactured the Linto Grand Prix Racer. Tonti's first task for his new employers had been to enlarge the original 703cc V-7 engine to 757cc, and then up to 844cc. But his own opinion was that all this was largely of secondary importance. It was the chassis design which was in need of an up-date.

His first problem lay in the height of the Guzzi twin engine between the cylinders. This was due to the position of the belt-driven generator on top of the crankcase, reflected in the tall timing cover casting at the front. Tonti solved this by substituting the generator with a Bosch GI(R) 14V 13A 19 alternator carried directly on the front of the crank. The distributor was changed for a Marelli S311A unit with twin contacts and condensers. With a suitably re-cast timing cover, this substantially reduced the overall height along the centre of the engine, allowing Tonti to then make his next move; the construction of a lower, lighter and far more rigid frame. And having detachable bottom frame rails meant engine removal was greatly simplified. Without a doubt, the design and the way it had been achieved displayed real engineering ability.

Besides using an alternator, in typical Guzzi fashion the only other significant engine modification on the V-7 Sport was a change in capacity.

In 1974, the V-7 gave way to the 750S. Clearly based on the original, there were a number of engineering changes as well as a restyling job. But the only really major change within the engine department was a move from gear drive in the timing case to a timing chain and sprockets. This was due more to cost than purely engineering considerations

The main reason for this was so that the factory could be allowed participation in 750cc production and Formula 750cc-type race events. The capacity chosen was 748.8cc, achieved by reducing the bore from 83mm of the 757cc version down to 82.5mm, while the stroke remained at 70mm.

In line with its sporting pretensions, higher compression, four-ring, 9.8:1 pistons were used, while a fiercer camshaft profile matched coiled valve springs; and 30mm Dell'Orto VHB 30 carbs completed the up-rating exercise, enabling the new engine to achieve 52bhp at 6300rpm.

In keeping with the other V-twins up to that time, the bores were in chrome, plated directly onto the alloy of cylinder castings, and again with matched piston assemblies.

The engine's drive train used a mix of the best parts from the 703, 757 and 844cc assemblies. And, like the newly-announced 850, the V-7 Sport featured a 5-speed gearbox. As on the earlier versions of the V-7 design, the gears were helically cut, mainly in the interest of quieter operation. Also new were the front forks – the first of the Guzzi models to use the type which were to be standard on the marques models from the mid-1970s onwards.

Although the 220mm drum brakes were retained from the earlier models, the front now sported one with twin leading shoes either side. This double-sided anchor did much to dispel the previous poor braking performance which was also assisted by weight reduction to 206kg (454lb).

The first supplies of the V-7 Sport began to roll off the Mandello production lines in early 1972. For 1973 the 850GT/GT California and V-7 Sport continued unchanged except for fresh colour schemes. But for the 1974 model year the V-7 Sport was dropped completely and it was the last year that the 850GT (or Eldorado as it was known in North America) and GT California were available. In this final year these models were fitted with a single 300mm cast iron disc, operated by a Brembo caliper, mounted at the front of the offside fork leg.

However, 1974 was important for another reason in the evolution of the large capacity Guzzi V-twin. This landmark was the 850T, a machine which was to transform both Guzzi's image and profitability on the world market by offering the running gear of the V-7 Sport (including the lower alternator-type engine) with the larger 844cc capacity.

Joining the 850T was the 750S. Both these models were the stepping stone to the best-selling 850T3, Le Mans, Spada and California T3 models which were soon to come.

Both the 850T and the 750S, besides sharing the same V-7 Sport-type chassis and forks, featured hydraulic disc front brakes, a single on the T, and a twin set up on the S. At the rear they both retained the 220mm drum, but now with 2LS operation.

The 850T's brakes were to be its chief weakness – and lead to the

introduction of the linked brake system triple disc 850T3 model. But 850T owners were unable to take action – an additional brake disc and caliper conversion kit was available as a spare part (part No. 17.92.30.00).

Except for the brakes (or lack of them), the 850T was very much a sports/tourer with 9.5:1 pistons, and the camshaft profile which was identical to the 750S (and the same as that used in the later Le Mans!). Once again the barrels and pistons were matched with the crankshafts and con-rods, colour-coded either blue or white. Together with 30mm VHB carbs, the 850T offered 53bhp, the same as the 750s but at 6000rpm against 6300rpm of the smaller engine. The only real significant change made in the engine compartment of the 850T/750S was to revert from the triple-gear drive in the timing case to the use of a cheaper timing chain and sprockets – a system used on the twins ever since.

Two other much smaller changes, but nonetheless important ones in the

Then in 1975 came the final development of the 750 sportster, in the shape of the S3. Although it was clearly based around the 750S, it used several major components for the new 850T3 touring model, including the patented linked brake system. The following year it was superseded by the first of the Le Mans series

evolution process, were the replacement of the threaded exhaust clamp with two studs on the exhaust port, only introduced on the 850T, not the 750S. And both models were to be the last of the line to employ the ancient (and inferior) wire-mesh oil filtration system introduced on the original V-7. All the later models carried a vastly more efficient car-type oil filtration cartridge.

Significantly, just before the 850T was taken out of production in 1975, the last batch constructed were fitted with the improved system, like the new models which commenced with the 850T3 and 750S3.

Touring

Whatever its sporting successes, the large capacity Moto Guzzi V-twins' real forté has always been in the touring sphere; providing an excellent blend of simplicity, reliability and economy, with a laid-back riding stance. Following on from the original V-7 touring mounts, the Mandello del Lario factory have continued to provide a never ending stream of practical long distance bikes, including the 850T/T3, V1000, 1000SP (Spada), T4 and T5, and the Mille GT, to name but a few.

The main difference between the 850T (described in Chapter 5) and its replacement, the T3, was in the braking department. It shared with other new-for-1975 models (T3 California and 750S3) Guzzi's exclusive patented integral triple-disc set-up. This was claimed to provide better stopping power and braking safety than any other conventional system.

Applying the footbrake pedal did not only operate the rear brake in the conventional way, but also it applied both the 242mm rear disc and the 300mm near-side front disc. The braking pressure was automatically balanced to produce bias needed to bring the rider to a steady, even stop. For emergencies, or simply to hold the bike while stationary, the front brake lever could also be used to apply the offside disc only. The front master cylinder had been substituted for one of a smaller capacity, which

The 850T replaced the 850GT during 1974. This introduced the V-7 Sport type chassis, together with alternator engine to Guzzis touring line. In many ways this was a landmark design, a machine which was to transform both image and the actual ability of what had, up to then, been a large capacity motorcycle of strictly limited appeal

The 1975 V1000 Convert was a revolutionary motorcycle, but one which ultimately proved a sales failure. Guzzi boss Alejandro De Tomaso misjudged the mood of the buying public, just as Honda did with their auto versions of the 400 twin and 750 four

had a plastic cap instead of the previous metal item. Unfortunately this was not an improvement because the cap proved damage-prone in service.

There were several other, if less significant, changes. Particular attention had been given to improving the oil and air filtration for the engine. The disposable car-type oil filter which made its début on the final batch of 850Ts was housed in sump, so that both this casting and its gasket were revised. And for the first time, the Dell'Orto carbs had a throw-away paper filter – vitally important for an engine employing chrome-plated cylinders which could not be rebored.

The Bosch alternator now had an increased output, at 280 watts. Although the headlamp remained an Aprilia product, it now featured a black, instead of chrome, shell. The American market model came with a sealed beam unit, much deeper rim, and a thick rubber gasket between the rim and shell. The idiot lights and instruments had a plastic console in place of the alloy type, and the ignition switch came with three instead of four positions. The clutch cable also incorporated a cut-out switch, which meant that the engine could not be started unless the lever was pulled in.

Other changes between the T and the T3 included handlebars, rear shocks, side panels, exhaust pipes and the design of the balance pipe running under the motor.

Later in the same year came the V1000 Convert. Unfortunately, despite being technically interesting, it was to prove a dismal sales failure. The reason that it is included here is because the V1000's combination of a large engine capacity, shaft final drive and automatic transmission made it

a unique bike at the time of its launch into the superbike era of the mid-1970s.

Subsequently, only mighty Honda, with special versions of the 400 twin and 750 four, have followed the same path. It has to be said that the Japanese company were no more successful in attracting customers to the concept than Guzzi. The Italian factory boss, Alejandro De Tomaso (an automobile man at heart) imagined that the 'luxury' fitment of the automatic tag would have the same impact as it does in the four-wheel world. Unfortunately he was to be proved wrong.

Like most automatic cars, the 'auto' Guzzi was closely based on an existing model, in this case the 850T3. As is often the case in the car world, the V1000 was provided with a larger displacement than the manual. The Convert (an inappropriate name!) also gained several touring extras, including the T3 California's tinted screen, panniers, footboards, side-stand and crash-bars. Outwardly, the only new parts were the grab rail, rear light and tail fairing, instrument console, front master cylinder and miniature aerofoils mounted on the front crash-bars; the real changes were out of sight, tucked away behind the engine and gearbox casings.

A total of twenty brand new 1000SP (Spada in Britain) models line up with the famous Guzzi wind tunnel as a backdrop during April 1978. This was the bike which the Italian factory saw as a viable alternative to BMW's R100RS in the long-haul, luxury touring market

The engine was essentially the same 90° V-twin which powered the 850 models with cylinder bore increased from 83mm to 88mm. With the stroke remaining the same as the 850's at 78mm, this gave the new engine a capacity of 948.80cc. On a 9.2:1 compression ratio, the maximum power output at the crankshaft was 71bhp at 6500rpm, but a lot less at the rear wheel, with the bought-in West German Sachs torque convertor consuming several bhp alone. Unlike the chromed bores of the earlier V-twins, the three-ring pistons of the Convert ran in steel cylinder liners. Although the factory still adhered to their method of matching the original pistons and cylinders on new machines, with Class 'A' between 88.000mm and 88.009mm, and Class 'B' from 88.009mm to 88.018mm, the use of steel liners meant that for the first time it was possible to rebore the V-twin engine. For this purpose, oversize piston assemblies were available in 0.4mm and 0.6mm.

The con-rods and crankshaft were the same type as the post-1972 850 engines, following a spate of broken rods which had resulted in the stroke being increased from 70mm to 78mm (with the introduction of the 850GT back in 1972); and similar care went into matching these at the factory, depending on the crankpin diameter. Factory markings were put on each con-rod and on the flywheel side of the crankshaft shoulder. Blue markings indicated a crankpin diameter of between 44.008 and 44.014mm, while white was for a pin between 44.094 and 44.020mm. Undersize split bearing shells were available in three sizes: 0.254mm, 0.508mm and 0.762mm. The remainder of the bottom end was virtually the same as on the 850, although the camshaft was modified to accommodate a drive for an automatic transmission fluid pump (the profile remained the same), and the timing cover was also modified. Because of cylinder bores, the crankcase mouths into which they fitted had to be enlarged, although the cylinder base gasket remained the same.

There was even less modification to the top end of the engine, just a new type of head gasket and different jets in the carburettors. And it is because of this that, in later years, many 850 Guzzis have been modified to 948cc V1000 capacity and above.

But on the V1000 all these changes were of course insignificant compared to what happened to the clutch and gearbox assembly. Strictly speaking, the system which Guzzi used was not a true automatic gearbox at all, but a form of semi-automatic transmission, based on a type of hydrokinetic torque convertor (hence I-Convert or Idro-Convert), bought in as a unit from the German Sachs company. This was fitted with a two-speed gearbox on which the ratios could be selected with a heel-and-toe lever operated by the left foot. To complicate matters there was also a clutch but its sole purpose was to swap between the two ratios, unlike a conventional gearbox, where it is also necessary for the clutch to be used

In designing the 1000SP, Guzzi engineers made full use of the factory's wind tunnel facilities. Several types of fairing were tried before the final shape was approved. This offered a good balance between style and function. Rider protection was good

Triking Cars of Norwich in Norfolk, constructed several sporting three-wheelers with the Guzzi V-twin as their power plant. Triking boss Tony Divey saw his product as very much a modern Morgan. The vehicle attracted attention wherever it went and, as on the Morgan, the engine was very much the central focus point. This particular example was constructed in 1983

to allow the engine to take up drive. On the V1000, this function was taken over completely by the torque convertor and since, in practice, changing ratio was virtually redundant, the machine was to most people as nearly automatic as to make no difference.

The Sachs torque convertor itself was a sophisticated development of what is sometimes known as a fluid flywheel (or, less politely, a slush box). These names are apt because they approximately describe its operation, in which the transmission medium is oil – a fluid. Instead of there being a direct link through the transmission, as in a conventional system, the fluid provides a slightly 'loose' connection and a gradual take-up – somewhat akin to the effect of slipping a friction clutch, but without the problems caused by doing this all the time. In effect, it provides a sort of continuously-variable transmission ratio, within the limits of the design specification.

On the V1000, the maximum converting ratio (akin to a gear ratio) was 1.60:1. The other end of the scale was direct 1:1 drive.

A separate convertor fluid tank had a capacity of 1.7 litres, and the recommended lubricant was Dextron ATF (automatic transmission fluid). The pressure in the system was controlled by a fluid pressure relief valve, located in the timing cover, adjacent to the convertor pump and calibrated to allow a running pressure of some 1.8-2kg/cm2 (25-29psi).

In practice, the net effect of this transmission system was too energy-sapping with the result that even with the extra cubes, maximum speed was reduced to only 108mph. This, allied to the strange feeling when riding the machine (like piloting an overlarge automatic moped), doomed the V1000 concept to the very backwaters of motorcycling. And in the end even Guzzi were forced to admit that the whole project had been a failure, and offered the V1000 in manual form as the G5 from 1978.

It was at the Milan Show in November 1977 that Guzzi enthusiasts were to witness the first benefits of the larger capacity of the V1000 on another model. This was a brand new concept for the Italian company, and one which owed a great deal to its northern German neighbour at BMW. This was the SP, known as the Spada (Sword) in Britain.

With the SP, Moto Guzzi set out to offer a viable alternative to BMW's virtual monopoly of the long haul, luxury touring market. For, although models such as the 850T3 were close to a BMW-style package, as a true competitor they fell short in several vital respects of the standard set by the top-of-the-range German flat twins. Most importantly, Guzzi (except the unpopular V1000) lacked the 1-litre engine capacity of the R100 series. They also lacked the sophistication that typified the Teutonic twins and, compared to the German company's range leader, the R100RS, lacked its purpose-built weather protection.

Guzzi power has also proved popular with sidecar enthusiasts, as this German visitor to the Isle of Man TT races proves. Main modifications usually include different forks, smaller wheels and sidecar gearing

Although a completely new concept, the SP was able to be put into production extremely quickly because it used, so far as the main chassis and engine parts were concerned, many components from the existing T3 and V1000 models. The increased engine capacity utilized the work already carried out to produce the '1000' class for the failed automatic, and this was simply given a conventional clutch and gearbox, courtesy of the T3, and housed in a frame and suspension package that again comprised of existing components from the 850 machine.

If these measures smacked of pure convenience engineering in order to boost the otherwise outclassed T3, this was because the bulk of the R&D budget was concentrated on those areas in which BMW dominated. Mandello's planners correctly perceived that their basic engine and chassis were sound enough, so it made both economic and practical sense to concentrate on those areas which Guzzi were currently not able to match BMW – in particular, rider protection.

Although the Spada's fairing was conceived in the factory's famous wind tunnel, it was not particularly aerodynamically efficient. The thinking behind the design was practical. The separate top section could turn with the handlebars, allowing it to be mounted much closer to the rider than a conventional fairing, which needs to be mounted far enough away to allow clearance for the handlebars on full lock. As a result, the Spada fairing offered an improved level of protection for the extremities of head and hands, areas which tended to be sacrificed for reasons of style or design compromise.

There was also a bonus in that the lower side panels (leg shields), which were firmly fixed to the frame, could be removed individually with very little effort and without the need to disturb the main top fairing. This greatly simplified routine engine maintenance work.

With a maximum speed pushing 120mph, superb rider protection and miserly fuel thirst – and at a cheaper price than BMW – Guzzi appeared to have a winner. Unfortunately there were also a number of negative points. These included a less than perfect fit of the fairing panels and poor design of the fittings, a less than comfortable dual seat and a combination of wafer-thin chrome-plate and less than perfect paintwork.

All this resulted in less sales than there should have been, and a mass of disgruntled owners who had taken the plunge and purchased an SP.

Eventually all this filtered through to the 'powers that be' at Mandello; the result being the SPNT (New Type), introduced in early 1980. This

Besides providing its rider with excellent protection from the elements, the 1000SPIII also has a comprehensive instrumentation, including speedo, rev counter, voltmeter and clock

was hardly a new bike, rather what the original should have been in the first place. In fact, at first inspection, except for a new set of colours and new 'flat' low-line Lafranconi silencers, the NT didn't look much different from the old SP. However, all this changed when one cocked a leg and actually went for a ride. For a start, the seat was now in the 'armchair' comfort league, the fairing had been improved in both fit and increased screen height, the former knee-crunching pads had been modified, the new silencers were more effective; and perhaps most important of all, the quality of the finish was much improved. Other differences included double-skinned exhaust pipes, Nicasil cylinder bores, and several more minor modifications.

The SP remained unchanged in this form until the end of 1983, when the SPII arrived. This was substantially altered in many important areas, including the angular cylinder head and barrel framing (with internal

modifications) introduced on the Le Mans III. There were also different wheels, brake discs and wider section tyres. Much of the cosmetics came from the T5 (which replaced the T4 at the same time). Also, like the T5, the SPII came with a 16in front wheel, very much a case of styling and trend rather than function and fact. Put simply, the 16in front wheel might have worked for certain racer replica Japanese hardware, but on the traditional twin shock Guzzi it was an absolute disaster. My only comment is, did anyone actually ride a prototype with this set-up before production was authorized? If so, that person should have been shot!

Of course, as with other mistakes, this was eventually put right, the result being the SPII 18in front wheel. The 1000 SP continued in this guise until it was replaced by the considerably different SPIII for the 1988 model year, and was made available with or without fuel injection.

The final segment of the large capacity Guzzi touring story is the Mille GT. Introduced in 1989, it owed much to the Le Mans sportster, but was very much a modern-day T3. It was available with both cast or the more traditional spoked wheels.

Above

Latest in the long line of large capacity Moto Guzzi touring motorcycles, the 1994 1000 Strada

Left

This 1000S, seen on Douglas Promonade, Isle of Man, in June 1993, sports a full fairing, cast alloy wheels (factory option), cylinder head protector bars and a rear carrier

Le Mans

Together with Ducati's original bevel-driven 900SS, Laverda's Jota and the MV Agusta America, the Moto Guzzi Le Mans rates as one of the great Italian classics of the 1970s – and unlike all the others, it was to survive not only into the 1980s, but creep into the 1990s as well.

Although the Le Mans made its public début at the Milan Show in November 1975, customers could not buy one until the following year. The Le Mans took its name from the famous French circuit and was clearly aimed at the same breed of sporting rider who would also be looking at a Ducati or Laverda – it scored on its more civilized manners, rendering it much more suitable to those who wanted something which could double as a tourer, as well as having the added advantage of shaft final drive.

Technically, the Le Mans (or 'Lemon', as it was often nicknamed) drew heavily on the 750S3 and 850T3. In fact, the engine assembly and transmission was essentially a tuned version of the 'cooking' T3; with identical cylinder dimensions, gearbox and final drive. To achieve the extra zip needed in its new role, the Le Mans came with higher dome three-ring pistons (10.2:1 compression), larger diameter valves (37mm exhaust, 44m inlet), a lumpier cam profile, and a pair of 36mm Dell'Orto

The original Le Mans I was a classic of 1970s Italian motorcycling. Together with the likes of the Ducati 900SS, Laverda Jota and MV Agusta America, the Le Mans set new standards in the Superbike arena. These were the days when Italy could build bikes to match the best from Japan – in performance, handling and braking, if not fit and finish

Available in red or the blue shown here, the Le Mans II replaced the original model in 1978. Its most obvious change was the adoption of an SP-style three-piece fairing, which gave the bike a more angular look

pumper carbs complete with large plastic bellmouths. Factory sources quoted 81bhp and 134mph, but omitted to say that this was with the Works production racing kit. Performance in standard trim was somewhat less spectacular: 71bhp at 124mph. Figures of 14 seconds and 98.9mph for the standing quarter-mile were hardly impressive, but at least some of these figures can be explained by overall high gearing and the closeness of the five gearbox ratios. An even closer look revealed that a full second was lost on the initial start, which with an additional 4mph at the end of the run related to a more respectable figure.

Thanks to its compact riding stance, razor sharp handling and excellent brakes, the Le Mans was able (with the factory race kit) to clock up a number of impressive production race victories which culminated in Roy Armstrong taking the 1977 Avon Championship (the top event in Britain at the time for sports bikes).

Another feature of the Le Mans was a pleasant loping gait, even at higher speeds. This was thanks to the high top gear ratio of 4.37:1, making the Italian V-twin far less hectic at maximum rpm than the busy nature of the conventional across-the-frame Japanese four-cylinder models of the period. All this gave the Le Mans a pleasant long-legged feel, making progress deceptively fast.

For a sportster, the electricals also came in for praise. A 1976 test in the respected journal *Motor Cycle* commented: 'The basic electrical gear on the Le Mans should be a model for other manufacturers too. A massive 280 watt alternator sits on the front of the crankshaft and feeds a monster

32 amp hour battery.' (Most bikes came with a less powerful 20 amp hour type). But tester John Nutting also found the finish wanting: 'So, under the skin the Le Mans is a motorcycle of indisputable quality. The surface lets it down, for the finish is very poor. The seat, a single moulding in foam rubber, split soon after the bike was picked up. The lining on the tank soon peeled after fuel was spilled on it, and the matt of the exhaust pipes was soon tarnished.' Nutting's comments regarding the seat were spot on – virtually every single Le Mans sold in 1976 had to have its seat replaced under warranty. The problem was that the seat was in fact a single rubber moulding which, as soon as it became hard through use, started to crack. This was cured by the following year, but many owners still chose to purchase a 750S3 component which fitted straight on, and looked nicer into the bargain.

The *Motor Cycle* test concluded with the following statement: 'This bike

Performance of the I and II were virtually the same, as were the Dell'Orto 36mm pumper carburettors with their large plastic bellmouths. Although a production racing kit (81 bhp) fitted, the Le Mans could best 135mph, in standard form (71 bhp) its top whack was 124 mph

The Le Mans III first appeared in 1981, an example of which is seen here at the Milan Show that year, and was a major redesign in its own right

has plenty to offer the competitive sporting rider. If he is able to overlook the wrinkles, then the road rider too should be rewarded with the basic integrity of the Guzzi Le Mans.'

Another internationally-important show heralded the MkII variant of Guzzi's best-selling Le Mans sportster. This was at the German Cologne event in September 1978. To many, though, the more angular lines of the MkII were a retrograde move. The most obvious change was the adoption of an SP-derived three-piece full fairing, which although offering increased rider protection, robbed the machine of its aggressive look. At the same time, the Le Mans gained most of the fairing-mounted goodies seen on the SP. These consisted of the complete instrumentation and switchgear, including the quartz clock and volt meter. Like the 1000SP, the Le Mans II featured a large (ugly!) moulded rubber dashboard. And, again like the SP, the front indicators were now integral to the fairing, whilst the clip-ons were changed to suit the fairing's upper section. Power output and performance largely remained unchanged.

In the autumn of 1980, a number of notable modifications were introduced on the Le Mans II. Firstly, the chrome-plated cylinders were superseded by Nickasil ones. At the same time the internal sealed fork dampers (which had proved less than satisfactory in service) were up-dated, and the forks themselves converted to air-assisted operation. Rear suspension was already altered, with Paiolo units now being specified.

A quite interesting fact is that no MkII reached the USA. Instead, a special model – the CX100 – was introduced in 1980 and continued

through into 1981. This was essentially a MkII chassis with a 1000cc SP engine.

When the Le Mans III took its bow in 1981, it was no simple cosmetic styling exercise; there were also internal changes. The engine in particular received engineering input in a way not seen on the earlier Marks. Instantly noticeable were the entirely new square-finned cylinder heads and matching Nickasil-plated cylinder barrels. Although such fundamentals as the camshaft profile and valve diameters remained unaltered, and even though the compression ratio was actually softened from 10:2 to 9.8:1 (to produce improved low speed response), the power output was still improved by a full 3bhp, with engine torque figures increased to 7.6kg/m at 6200rpm.

The increase in power output was the result of superior machining equipment allowing closer tolerances, the use of aluminium rocker

Also available in silver, the Le Mans III sported a new fairing, tank, seat, panels, exhaust system and engine changes. But although the swinging arm was lengthened, the frame, forks and wheel basically remained unaltered

Side panel of the 850 Le Mans III. These were badges rather than decals, a tradition carried forward from the earlier versions

supports (which also quietened the tappets), an improved air filter, and finally changes to the exhaust system. The latter was in fact the first to meet a stringent new European regulation; but, cleverly, Guzzi engineers managed to combine noise requirement with improved performance.

The fairing was another component to receive major attention, and a new design (tested in Guzzi's on-site facilities) featured considerably reduced dimensions. There was a form of spoiler, its purpose being to deflate air past the base of the fuel tank and the top of the cylinder heads. Other changes included a new 100mm white-face Veglia rev counter which took pride of place on the instrument board; new tank, seat and side panels; new footrest support brackets, and front direction indicators. Less noticeable, but a considerable improvement, was the headlamp which boasted a first-class quartz H4 assembly and at last provided the Le Mans with adequate night-time vision.

The next cycle in the LM evolution came in late 1984 with the début of the Le Mans 1000 (more often referred to simply as the 'MkIV'). This shared the larger 948.8cc (88 x 78mm) motor already used in the California II and SPII models, but in a higher state of tune. Differences included 3mm larger diameter valves (both inlet and exhaust) than on the 850 engine, a higher (10:1) compression ratio, bigger (40mm) Dell'Ortos and new exhaust pipes of the same diameter. The mufflers were also of a different type, and both these and the header and balance pipes were finished in a gloss black chrome-plating.

With these changes, the power output rose to 86bhp at the crankshaft

Left

A Le Mans III at rest besides a tortuous Italian mountain road. With its torquey engine, safe handling and triple Brembo discs, it was well able to give a good account of itself in such arduous conditions

Above

Most noticeable of the III's engine changes was the introduction of new, square finned cylinder heads and Nickasil coated barrels. Other differences included a lower compression ratio, the use of aluminium rocker supports and an improved air filtration and exhaust system

(worth slightly less than 80bhp by the time it was measured at the rear wheel), whilst top speed jumped by over 10mph giving the new Le Mans 140mph potential.

As for styling, the MkIV drew heavily on the then current V65 Lario, itself inspired by the V35 Imola II, and its brother the V50 Monza II. Fashion (Japanese variation) meant a belly pan below the top half fairing, and a 16in front wheel. The latter innovation was to prove a disastrous one by the Guzzi management; it might have suited the lighter, quicker-turning Japanese hardware of the period, but Guzzi's big V-twin – no!

Except for the substitution of an 18in front wheel in 1987, the MkIV continued virtually unchanged until it was finally pensioned-off in the early 1990s – the last of the 1970s Italian superbikes to survive, and a lasting tribute to the basic credentials of the original concept.

Left

The view most other riders got of the Le Mans III; certainly on a tight, twisty road where handling prowess and bottom end power counted for more than outright horsepower. Lakeside view is typical of those around Lake Como near Mandello del Lario

Above

The next move in the Le Mans saga came in late 1984 with the debut of the Le Mans 1000. Like the earlier V1000, SP and California II, this used 948.8cc version of the V-twin, but with a higher state of tune to justify the LM tag. Styling (a 1986 model is shown) was very much in vogue of the V65 Lario four-valve sportster, introduced a few months earlier. Note 16 inch front wheel

Right

By 1988 the factory had come to their senses and installed an 18 inch front wheel and, with it, its handling prowess. Ever-popular Italian racing red was one colour choice …

Above

… the other this smart black finish with gold pinstriping and white cast alloy wheels. Performance of the Le Mans 1000 (often called the Mark IV) was 141mph. The valves were 3mm larger in diameter than on the 850, higher compression ratio (10:1) and larger 40mm carburettors

Smaller Vees

The German Cologne Show in September 1976 witnessed the public's first glimpse of a range of middleweight Guzzi V-twins which were to play a pivotal role in the Italian marque's fortunes over the remainder of the decade, into the 1980s, and one which is still important today.

Alejandro De Tomaso realized that if he was ever to build the famous old company back to its former glory, production figures would have to rise dramatically, and the range of models head downwards into the lightweight and middleweight areas of the markets. However, the Benelli-based four-cylinder models (350 and 400 GTS) introduced in 1974 had proved a solid failure in the efforts to motivate showroom success. So de Tomaso realized that what worked for the Japanese didn't necessarily work for the Italian bike industry. With this in mind, it is perhaps unsurprising that, instead, he chose to instruct chief designer Lino Tonti to craft a smaller version of the heavyweight V-twin which had done so well for the company. The result, at first emerging as the V35 and V50, was everything which de Tomaso could have wished for; essentially a scaled-down recreation of the classic 90° V-twin ohv four-stroke with shaft, final drive and twin front downtube frame (the latter in which nearside bottom frame tube was detachable, again as on the bigger original).

The V50 (shown) and V35 middleweight V-twins made their public bow at the German Cologne Show in September 1976. Here was, for the first time, a Guzzi V-twin intended for the mass market

Part of the original V50 colour brochure showing various aspects of the machine including: engine assembly, switchgear, instrumentation, throttle control and brakes

To meet the hoped-for demand it was soon decided to transfer production of the new middleweights from Mandello del Lario to the former Innocenti plant in Milan, from which hundreds of thousands of Lambretta scooters had been built to see service the world over during the 1950s and 1960s.

Milanese V35/50s started to be built in the autumn of 1978 (coded II for the larger model); in other words the 1979 model year. The large jump in production capacity offered by the former Innocenti facilities gave Guzzi the chance to slingshot its new middleweight (at least in 500 form) right up there with the Japanese. Its closest rival was Honda's new CX500 V-twin. Not only was the V50 a much lighter design that the Japanese bike, but on some markets – notably Britain – it also undercut on price.

During 1979 a series of road test reports in the motorcycling press hailed the V50 as simply the best middleweight in the world. Typical was the

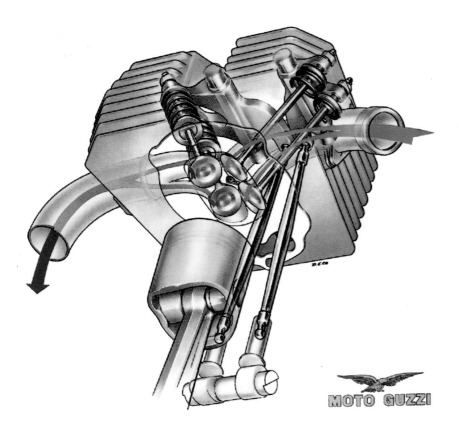

Motor Cycle News headline: 'It's got the lot!'. Unfortunately the V50II's service record was to prove something different, as many dealers (including myself) were to discover to our cost.

The reality was a catalogue of warranty problems including poor paintwork, problematic electrics (particularly the ignition switch), oil seal failures in both the final drive shaft flange and front forks, not to mention an incurable flat spot which was due to the crankshaft-mounted electronic ignition trigger.

After all the press hype and record sales levels for an Italian V-twin (over 2000 examples were sold in the UK alone during 1979), it was a major embarrassment that the V50II didn't live up to expectations. So in mid-1980 the improved MkIII took its bow.

Much of the earlier models' faults had been rectified. Unfortunately the damage to Guzzi's name had already been done and sales were well down on 1979 levels. Even so, it is worth mentioning the improvements: better finish (including replacement of the original rust-prone steel front mudguard with a plastic component, larger diameter valves, increased choke diameter, improved exhaust and inlet porting, a less restrictive

*The Japanese-only V40 Capri;
essentially a 350 Imola II with an
increase in capacity. Besides the 4-valve
heads, other notable features included
16 inch wheels, flipped up rear seat
section, bikini fairing, belly pan and red
wheels. Maximum speed was almost
105mph*

exhaust system, a halogen headlamp, revised electrics (including switches!)
and lighter steering, thanks to the brake calipers being moved from front
to rear of the fork sliders.

But the biggest single change was hidden away under the circular cover
at the front of the engine. The MkII's troublesome electronic ignition had
disappeared to be replaced by old-fashioned twin contact breakers and twin
condensers, whilst the simplex cam chain gave way to a most robust duplex
device with a spring-loaded tensioner.

Generally speaking, the V35/50 series shared identical external
dimensions, but a bore and stroke of 66 x 50.6mm for the smaller unit
against 74 x 57mm for the V50, and gave capacities of 346.23cc and
490.30cc respectively.

The cylinder bores were Nickasil-coated, with piston/cylinder pairings of
A, B or C codings. The three-ring pistons were unusual in featuring
concave crowns; this resulted from the cylinder head design which Tonti
and his engineering team had chosen. Instead of the conventional
hemispherical combustion chamber and angled valves, the inside of the
head was flat, with both valves parallel. Space for combustion was instead
provided in the top of the piston itself, rather than the head.

Although an innovation for Moto Guzzi, the 'Heron combustion layout',
as it was named, had already been well proven on both cars (Jaguar) and
bikes (Morini) amongst others.

Twin coil springs were specified for each valve, which operated in an
iron guide, retained in the head by a circlip.

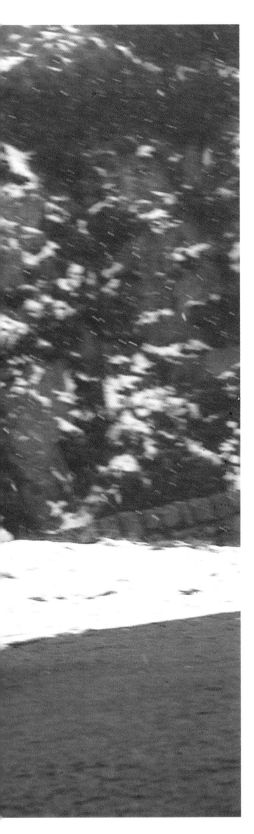

A distinctive feature of the middleweight Guzzi V-twin engine was the square finning of both the cylinder heads and barrels. There were also anti-resonance rubber blocks similar to those fitted to many air-cooled two-strokes to reduce fin ringing.

The crankcase, unlike the larger vees, was in two sections, split horizontally and retained as a pair by ten studs of varying length. The one-piece crankshaft carried a pair of bolt-up steel connecting rods with 15mm gudgeon pins running in bronze small-end bushes. Again, there were Class 'A' (blue) and Class 'B' (white) con-rods which had been factory matched to crankshafts of the same coding.

The motor was lubricated in a similar fashion to the larger vees, with a lobe-type pump, circulating oil throughout the engine. However, the car-type canister filter was mounted externally, allowing easier removal.

Again, the transmission was similar, but not quite the same. As on the

Above

An interesting prototype which never made it to production, the 350 Falco was displayed at the Milan Show in November 1987. Underneath the bodywork it was essentially a V35 Imola II, but with conventional 2-valve heads

Left

The bike which should have been a winner but wasn't; the V75. Launched in 1985 it suffered from the 4-valve head troubles, a 16 inch front wheel which didn't help the handling and a poorly designed fairing

larger capacity models, the clutch was to be found inside the large-diameter ring gear for the electric starter. But an important difference was the clutch – a single-plate diaphragm-type, consisting of a friction plate, pressure cap, pressure plate and diaphragm spring.

The 5-speed constant-mesh gearbox featured frontal engagement, with a nearside foot lever. Internal ratios were identical for both the V35 and V50. Another variation was the use of straight cut, rather than the helical, gears of the bigger V-twins. Other features included a one-piece alloy swinging arm, 35mm diameter front fork tubes, 12-spoke cast-alloy wheels and the

by-now-familiar patented linked brake system. Sporting versions in the shape of the Imola (350) and Monza (500) were also offered. But although they looked pretty, performance was little different from the standard models.

More developments saw the production of the V35II (1980), V65 (1982), Imola II, Monza II and V65 Lario (1984), V35II (1986) and V-75 (1985). Some of these newcomers featured 4-valve heads, but unfortunately this once again led to a spate of warranty-associated difficulties (although a successful answer was eventually found). Both the V35II and V-75 were generally disliked; the larger bike in particular proving a major flop.

In typical Guzzi fashion, development was the order of the day, not outright new design. So appeared the 750 Targa, 750SP, 750T and others which have survived until today in revised form, although in the 1990s all versions are seen as basic, even crude by most observers.

Custom Cruisers

Ever since the first Guzzi custom bike – the original California of the early 1970s – laid-back American street cruisers have figured in the Mandello del Lario factory's marketing strategy. And when British importers Three Cross announced their 1994 line-up, the least expensive of the Italian V-twins was the 350 Nevada custom at £3699.

That first 'Cali' was essentially a 1972 850 GT dressed with a number of accessories, including a comprehensive toughened perspex screen hi and wide bars, a wide two-colour custom seat adorned with a chrome-plated rail, fibreglass panniers, rear carrier, front and rear crash-bars, and finally a pair of footboards instead of conventional footrests for the rider.

Always a popular model, the new California II made its bow in the 1981 model year. This shared the engine's basic changes, with the Le Mans III introduced at the same time. This example is stock, except for abbreviated non-standard drag pipes

Together with the GT, the California was up-dated for the 1974 model year with a single 300mm cast iron Brembo disc, replacing the original drum brake. The success of this machine led Guzzi to offer a California version of the new 850T3 in 1975. Not only did the new custom benefit from an improved frame and forks, but also triple disc brakes with Guzzi patented integral system, and a weight-saving of some 30kg (66lb). Once again, it came equipped with all the usual goodies – a major selling point – and it sold well against standard models.

When a brand new California, the II took its bow at the Milan Show in November 1981, it proved a strange mixture of old and new, with a return to an appearance not dissimilar to the original 850GT California of the early 1970s, while its motor was updated by utilizing the square 'slab'-style cylinder heads and barrels first employed on the Le Mans III. Like the Le Mans III, the new machine was substantially different from the bike it replaced. Not only was its detail, specification and appearance altered, but its engine capacity was enlarged to 948.81cc. This placed the California in the 1-litre category, achieved in precisely the same way as it had been with the V1000, G5 and SP models – by scooping out the bore to 88mm.

Guzzi claimed a maximum speed of 118mph, but in truth the Cali III was barely able to breast 105mph. Not only this, but at around 90mph, or occasionally somewhat less, depending upon exact road and weather conditions, an unsettling weave would set in. It must, however, be pointed out that this can also be a problem with other makes using a large perspex windscreen, but at lower speeds the benefits outweigh the problems.

In the late 1980s the III became the 1000 and was ultimately offered with both conventional 30mm Dell'Orto carbs and a digital electronic Weber fuel injection system. Both options were available in LAPD (Los Angeles Police Department) replica, FF (fully-faired) forms, and both cast wheels or wire wheels could be specified.

When the V35 and V50 models first appeared at the end of the 1970s, it didn't take the factory long to offer custom versions (at least for the domestic market); the first model being the V35C (Custom, not California). From this initial venture was to stem a whole line of smaller V-engined American custom cruisers, including the V50C, V65C, V35 Florida, V65 Florida, 350 Nevada and 750 Nevada. Of these, the most radical was the Nevada but, even so, both versions shared much of the basics with their roadster brethren.

Above

California III arrived in 1988. Actually, it was for the engine capacity being increased from 844 to 948cc; a 1991 Milan Show California III with unusual colour scheme and brown saddle

Left

The V65 Florida was available either naked or with the screen, panniers carrier and crashbars shown here. A V35 version was also built, but this was not imported into Britain

Above

Another of the company's exhibits at the 1991 Milan Show was this striking white 350 Nevada, the latest in a long line of Moto Guzzi custom bikes. Although many of the cycle parts were new, the basic mechanics could be traced all the way back to the first V35 of 1977

Right

The other Nevada was the 750. Specification includes a pair of PUBH 30mm Dell'Orto carbs, spoked wire wheels (18in front, 16in rear) laced to alloy rims, a 17 litre fuel tank, 177 kg dry weight and 106 mph top speed

Left
From the 1994 model year, the California became the 1100. Once again there were various options, including this basic model with wire wheels and no panniers or screen

Above
Fully-faired 1000 California (Mark III) was available with either carburettors (shown) or digital electronic injection Weber IAW ALFA-N system, with electric feeding pump. The choice of cast alloy or spoked wheels is also available

Magni

For over a quarter of a century, Arturo Magni was a familiar figure in the Grand Prix paddocks from the start of the official World Championship series, way back in 1949. In fact, as one journalist once put it, "Arturo Magni has probably seen more classic motorcycle races than any other man alive". Although today he is widely known for his beautiful Guzzi V-twin-powered creations, this was not always the case, as for many years he was the driving force behind the famous MV Agusta race effort, both as team manager and in charge of race preparations for a string of champions including the likes of Ubbiali, Surtees, Hocking, Hailwood, Agostini and Read.

Born near the Gilera factory in Arcore, in his youth Arturo was a keen aero modeller and this led to a strong friendship with Ferruccio Gilera, son of the boss of the famous marque. So, when he was made redundant after the war, when the aircraft plant in which he was employed folded in 1947, it was a natural step into the Gilera racing department. In 1950 he quit Gilera to join the then fledgling MV team at their Cascina Costa factory near the Gallarate headquarters; an association which was to be a highly successful one for both parties. From then, until MV pulled out of racing in 1977, they set up the fabulous record of 37 Manufacturers and 38 Rider world road racing titles. following the factory's closure, Magni worked for a short period as a consultant for the former German MV importer who produced a small number of specials, including the 1000 Ago and 1100 GP – all based around the final MV production models. In addition, he also started an organization to market MV tuning goodies and frame kits.

In 1980 Arturo Magni made his first move away from total reliance on MV, with a frame kit to house the Honda CB900 unit. Called the MH1, it not only used the Japanese engine but also Honda forks, swinging-arm, shock absorbers, brakes and the exhaust system. Built exclusively for export, in 1981 Magni produced a total of 150 MH1s and the later MH2s.

An important machine made its public debut at the Cologne Show staged in September 1982. This was the MB2, powered by a flat-twin BMW engine, and the success of the Magni BMW led to the introduction three years later of the Magni team's latest creation, the Le Mans, shown at Milan in November 1985. The Le Mans took as its power unit the

Arturo Magni's first Guzzi-powered offering was the Magni Le Mans and was shown to the public for the first time at the Milan Show in November 1985. It was available with a choice of 948 or 1116cc capacities

Testing the Magni Le Mans (the first British journalist to do so, in the July 1986 issue of Motorcycle Enthusiast*) I commented 'At £5750 for the 1000 and an extra £300 for the 1100, the Magni Le Mans cannot be said to be cheap, but for this sum you do get the chance to own one of the world's most exclusive and exciting motorcycles'*

Above

Also available was this Magni Parallelogram conversion kit for standard Guzzi models

latest 1000 (actually 948.8cc) V-twin engine from Moto Guzzi – also available exclusively from Magni as an 1100 (1116.87cc).

Testing one of these machines in the July 1986 for *Motorcycle Enthusiast*, I commented: 'At £5750 for the 1000 and an extra £3000 for the 1100, the Magni Le Mans cannot be said to be cheap, but for this sum you do get the chance to own one of the world's most exclusive and exciting motorcycles, built by someone who has managed to pack more motorcycle experiences into his life than most of us can dream about.'

Unlike previous Magni offerings, the Le Mans was only available as a complete machine, not as a separate frame kit. Moto Guzzi supplied the engine unit, exhaust system and rear drive box directly to the Magni organization. The only other parts found on both the production Guzzi Le Mans and the Magni were the twin Dutch Koni rear shocks. Everything else was either produced in-house or obtained from new. With the Le Mans, Elaborazioni Magni could truly be said to have come of age as a full motorcycle manufacturer in its own right.

By 1991, the Magni Guzzi range had been extended to include the Classico 1000, Arturo 1000, Sfida 1000 and 350, Sfida Ottovalvole ie

(4-valve fuel injection), the Le Mans 1000 and Australia.

There were also kits to transform the standard Guzzi big V-twin to Parallelogram swinging arm, and an 1100cc kit (as used on the big-bore Magni Le Mans). The Classico was available with wire or cast alloy wheels. The most glamorous – and fastest – of the Magni Guzzis is the Australia with its 992cc (90 x 78mm) Daytona motor and Weber Marelli fuel injection. The Australia sprang from a co-operation between Magni and Ted Stolarski of Transport Holdings Pty Limited of Western Australia. Built purely as a racing bike, its initial outing was Daytona in March 1990. Due to very little testing, the team were pleased to finish the Battle of the Twins race within the first 20 – out of a field of more than 40 starters.

A mere two weeks later, the Magni Australia Prototype took third in the Heavyweight Twins class at Roebling Road raceway; and finally a first in the same division at West Palm Beach, Florida. All these races were contested against a strong international and American field. The rider was the experienced Australian superbike rider, Owen Coles.

Upon its return to Australia, the machine was ridden by New Zealander Simon Turner, not just in Battle of the Twins racing (known as 'BEARS' in New Zealand, and 'Thunderbikes' in Australia), but also the Superbike class where it often beat the very latest Japanese four-cylinder models.

This initial prototype used the old two-valve motor and carburetters, but later it was fitted with the Daytona engine and fuel injection, and it is in this form that the bike is now available for purchase as part of the 1994 Magni line-up.

Simon Turner sums it up in the following manner: 'Having ridden the Magni-framed Guzzi in different types of events, one thing has become clear. It's a very effective motorcycle. The Guzzi engine provided a perfect match for the Magni frame, and proved very strong and reliable. With the shaft drive virtually unnoticeable because of the parallelogram system, my exit speeds from corners were always superior to that of my competitors. In summary I must say that the Magni Guzzi is as enjoyable to ride as it is effective on the track.'

With such an accolade, no wonder Arturo Magni and his products are held in such high esteem by enthusiasts around the world.

Above far right

In response to a more traditional machine, Magni and his son Giovanni launched the Le Mans Classic in 1987. This had all the benefits of the normal Magni Le Mans, plus the advantage of looking as if it had come from the 1970s with its timeless style

Above right, and below

Following the success of both the Magni Le Mans and Le Mans Classic came the Sfida 1000; this time aimed very much at the cafe race brigade with its abbreviated fairing, clip-ons, rear sets, upswept silencers and racing tank and seat. (Photograph below, David Goldman)

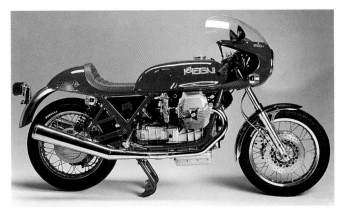

One of the most outstanding features of the various Magni Guzzis is the unusual
rear fork. It uses a double (parallelogram) swinging arm which pivots on self-
lubricating ball-joints, but unlike many modern machines used twin rear shock
absorbers. Based on a system tried on the racing MV Agustas of the early 1950s,
this system is claimed to largely eliminate the problems of torque reaction with shaft
final drive, the swinging arm working independently from the rear drive, which
itself features twin fully floating universal joints

The original racing-only Magni-Australia on show at Milan in 1991. This stemmed from co-operation between Arturo Magni and Ted Stolarski of Transport Holdings Pty Ltd of Western Australia. Early riders included Owen Coles and Simon Turner. From 1994 the Australia became an integral part of the Magni line-up

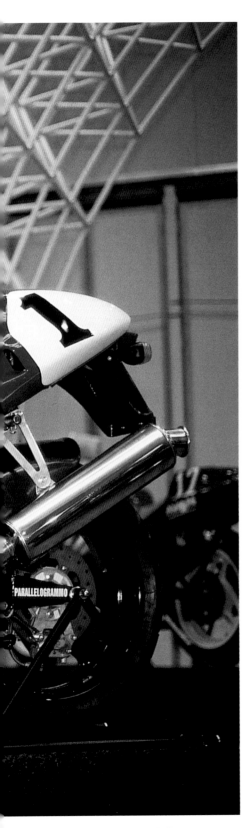

Above

Front end of Magni Australia showing twin pot Brembo racing brake caliper, fully floating disc, carbon-fibre mudguard/fork protector and Pirelli Dragon 17 inch radial tyre

Left

Specification of the Magni Australia includes a capacity of 992cc (90 x 78mm) and Marelli fuel injection. This example was photographed by Terry Howe at the National Exhibition Centre, Birmingham, in October 1993 and is in road, not racing trim

Daytona

Even the most ardent Guzzi enthusiast had been wondering if the Mandello concern would ever build its long-promised production version of the Dr John racing team's successful Battle of the Twins racer.

These prayers were finally answered in November 1991 at the Milan Show, and the good news was that the red Daytona 1000 was not only ready but well worth the wait. It is perhaps ironic that a former dentist (hence the 'Dr John' title) from Philadelphia, USA, should be the man to put Moto Guzzi back on the map. But that's exactly what has happened. John Wittner is a lifelong motorcycle buff who took up dentistry after training in engineering, only to throw it all in to go endurance racing with a group of like-minded individuals, and finally contact Guzzi boss Alejandro de Tomaso about securing backing for an all-new racing chassis.

The Dr John race team had its first major success by winning the US Endurance Championship in the successive years of 1984 and 1985. Rider Doug Brauneck won the US Pro-Twins title in 1987. De Tomaso was so impressed by these achievements that he gave Wittner a prototype eight-valve race engine designed by veteran engineer Umberto Todero who had been with the factory every since Guzzi's glory days on the 1950s. The resultant Wittner Guzzi racer scored a third place in its debut race in the 1988 Daytona twins event, and further leader-board position throughout that year saw Wittner invited to Mandello the following year to start work on a road-going version. Over two years later the Daytona 1000 was born.

The production bike utilizes a rectangular steel spine frame and cantilever swinging arm similar to that of the Dr John race bikes. Styling, however, is all fresh and considerably different from that found on the initial prototype back in 1989, with the 992cc air-cooled V-twin engine on display below the sculptured half fairing. The engine employs belt drive to activate each cylinder's single overhead camshaft. With around 100bhp on top, the Daytona is well able to give a good account of itself on road or track; and a factory tuning kit is available in Stage 1 or Stage 2 (basically one for fast road work, the other for competition only).

Compared to earlier versions of the big V-twin Guzzi theme, the Daytona is a considerable advance. Not just the four valves per cylinder single overhead cam with belt drive, but the much more 'modern feel' once under way. From the moment you lean forward to take up your riding stance with the low clip-ons, and fire-up the big V-twin, right through to the light throttle and light clutch actions, the differences between old and new are instantly recognizable. The throttle response is due to the Weber-Marelli fuel injection system. Not only this, but the

Opposite

Dr John Wittner with his brainchild, the Daytona 1000. (Photograph, Roland Brown)

Below

A Daytona on the company's stand at the 1991 Milan Show. At 205 kg dry, the Daytona is reasonably light for its capacity size, whilst the combination of a 17in front and 18in rear wheel, combined with modern geometry, give a much sportier, more flickable feel than the slow-steering Guzzis of yesteryear

Daytona is unexpectedly quiet, both mechanically and through its twin exhausts. It is in this area that much of the time-consuming development work went and the reason why development time was greater than many thought it should have been. For a small factory such as Guzzi, the effort to gain world-wide homologation was a major headache. With peak revs set at 8000rpm, it is good to know that maximum torque is produced further down the scale at 6000rpm. The abundance of low-rev and mid-range pulling-power make the standard Daytona a joy to ride. It also means there is no need for frequent use of the 5-speed box which, although it contains straight-cut cogs, is still a close relation of the original assembly found on other Guzzi Vees.

If the engine generally feels like a tuned variant of previous Guzzis, the chassis most definitely does not. At 205kg (420 lb) dry, the Daytona is reasonably light, and the combination of a 17in front and 18in rear wheel, combined with modern geometry, give a much sportier, more 'flickable feel' than the slow-steering Guzzis of yesteryear. This improved response is all the more impressive because it hasn't taken place at the expense of straight-line stability which is as good as ever. Much of this must be thanks to Wittner's parallelogram swinging arm linkage, which all but cures the usual shaft-drive torque reaction found on earlier Guzzi Vees.

Another departure from conventional Guzzi big twin practice are the Brembo brakes – independent, unlike the usual linked system. Suspension is taken care of by a pair of flex-free 41mm Marzocchi front forks and a multi-adjustable Koni rear shock. On this latter item, a key role is played by the stut's spring rate. This is critical because it acts as a counter to the dreaded shaft drive 'screwing' effect. Two springs are offered to provide customers with a choice when setting their bike up to particular needs of rider weight and road surfaces.

The end result is a machine of which Guzzi (and John Wittner) can be proud. A modern Guzzi for the 1990s, which it is hoped can achieve the same level of success for the Mandello factory as the original Le Mans I did in the 1970s.

Another Dr John Wittner-inspired bike is the new 1100 Sport. Clearly making use of the development work which went into the Daytona, this uses a larger capacity version of the conventional two-valve per cylinder ohv pushrod V-twin motor, rather than the Daytona's exotic four-valve per cylinder ohc unit. Guzzi themselves, and their dealers around the world, all consider this bike to have considerable sales potential. Only time will tell if they are right.

Definitive Daytona as it appeared in this studio shot on the eve of the Milan Show in November 1991

Above far right

Pre-production prototype of what was to emerge as the Daytona, as seen early in 1991. The whole project stemmed from the American Dr John Wittner's successful efforts with Guzzi V-twins in Stateside Battle of the Twins during the 1980s.

Below right

For those wanting the style of the Daytona, but without its high price tag, Guzzi provide the 1100 Sport. This first appeared in mid-1993 and looks set to be one of the firm's best sellers in 1994 and beyond

Specifications

Model	Normale	Sport 15	P175	PE250
Year	1921-24	1931-39	1932	1934-39
No cylinders	1	1	1	1
Bore (mm)	88	88	59	68
Stroke (mm)	82	82	63.7	64
Capacity (cc)	498.4	498.4	174	238
Compression ratio (tol)	4	4.5	5.5	5.5
Power: bhp	8	13.2	7	9
@rpm	3000	3800	4200	4000
Valve type	ioe	ioe	ohv	ohv
No gears	3	3	3	3
Front suspension	girder	girder	girder	girder
Rear suspension	rigid	rigid	rigid	spring & friction
Tyre size front	3.00x26	3.50x19	3.00x19	3x19
Tyre size rear	3.00x26	3.50x19	3.00x19	3x19
Dry weight (kg)	130	150	115	135

Model	GTW	Motoleggera	Airone Sport	Lodola 175
Year	1935-46	1946-54	1949-58	1956-58
No cylinders	1	1	1	1
Bore (mm)	88	42	70	62
Stroke (mm)	82	46	64	57.8
Capacity (cc)	498.4	64	247	174.5
Compression ratio (tol)	5.5	5.5	7	7.5
Power: bhp	22	2	12	9
@rpm	4500	5000	5200	6000
Valve type	ohv	rotary valve ts	ohv	ohc
No gears	4	3	4	4
Front suspension	girder	blade	teles	teles
Rear suspension	spring & friction	central spring	spring & friction	s/arm
Tyre size front	3.25x19	1.75x26	3.00x19	2.50x18
Tyre size rear	3.50x19	1.75x26	3.00x19	3.00x17
Dry weight (kg)	180	45	137	109

Model	Lodola	Zigolo 110	Stornello Sport	Dingo GT
Year	1959-66	1960-66	1961-68	1967-70
No cylinders	1	1	1	1
Bore (mm)	68	52	52	38.5
Stroke (mm)	64	52	58	42
Capacity (cc)	235	110.3	123.1	48.9
Compression ratio (tol)	7.5	7.5	8	7.5
Power: bhp	11	4.8	8.5	1.4
@rpm	6000	5200	7500	4800
Valve type	ohv	rotary valve ts	ohv	ts
No gear	4	3	4	4
Front suspension	teles	teles	teles	teles
Rear suspension	s/arm	s/arm	s/arm	s/arm
Tyre size front	2.50x18	2.50x17	2.50x17	2.00x18
Tyre size rear	3.00x17	2.75x17	2.50x1	2.00x18
Dry weight (kg)	115	78	92	48

Model	V7 700 Special	Falcone Nuovo	V7 Sport	V7
Year	1967-76	1969-76	1969-71	1972-74
No cylinders	2	1	2	2
Bore (mm)	80	88	83	82.5
Stroke (mm)	70	82	70	70
Capacity (cc)	703.7	498.4	757.5	748.4
Compression ratio (tol)	9	6.8	9	9.8
Power: bhp	40	26.2	45	52
@rpm	5800	4800	6000	6300
Valve type	ohv	ohv	ohv	ohv
No gears	4	4	4	5
Front suspension	teles	teles	teles	teles
Rear suspension	s/arm	s/arm	s/arm	s/arm
Tyre size front	4.00x18	3.50x18	4.00x18	3.25x18
Tyre size rear	4.00x18	3.50x18	4.00x18	3.50x18
Dry weight (kg)	234	214	228	206

Model	GT850	250TS	V1000	850 Le Mans
Year	1972-74	1974-82	1975-84	1976-84
No cylinders	2	2	2	2
Bore (mm)	83	56	88	83
Stroke (mm)	78	47	78	78
Capacity (cc)	844	231.5	948.8	844
Compression ratio (tol)	9.2	9.75	9.2	10.2 (1976-80) 9.8 (1981-84)
Power: bhp	51	24.5	50	71 (1976-80) 76 (1981-84)
@rpm	6000	7570	6250	7300 (1976-80) 6200 (1981-84)
Valve type	ohv	ts	ohv	ohv
No gears	5	5	automatic	5
Front suspension	teles	teles	teles	teles
Rear suspension	s/arm	s/arm	s/arm	s/arm
Tyre size front	4.00x18	3.00x18	100/90H18	100/90V18
Tyre size rear	4.00x18	3.25x18	110/90H18	110/90 V18
Dry weight (kg)	235	132	229	211 (1976-78) 220 (1978-80) 206 (1981-84)

Model	V35 (original)	V50 (original)	125 2C4T	V65 (original)
Year	1977-79	1977-79	1979-83	1981-85
No cylinders	2	2	2	2
Bore (mm)	66	74	45.5	80
Stroke (mm)	50.6	57	38	64
Capacity (cc)	346.2	490.3	123.57	643.4
Compression ratio (tol)	10.8	10.8	10.65	10
Power: bhp	27	45	16.3	52
@rpm	7750	7500	1100	7050
Valve type	ohv	ohv	ohc	ohv
No gears	5	5	5	5
Front suspension	teles	teles	teles	teles
Rear suspension	s/arm	s/arm	s/arm	s/arm
Tyre size front	90/90x18	100/90x18	2.75x18	100/90 H18
Tyre size rear	3.00x18	100/90x18	3.00x18	110/90 H18
Dry weight (kg)	152	168	110	165

Model	750 Targa	1000 Quota	1000 California Injection	Daytona
Year	1988-92	1990-	1990-	1992-
No cylinders	2	2	2	2
Bore (mm)	80	88	88	90
Stroke (mm)	74	78	78	78
Capacity (cc)	743.9	948.8	948.8	992
Compression ratio (tol)	9.7	9.5	9.2	10
Power: bhp	59	7	72	90
@rpm	7000	6500	6500	7500
Valve type	ohv	ohv	ohv	ohc
No gears	5	5	5	5
Front suspension	teles	teles	teles	teles
Rear suspension	s/arm	s/arm	s/arm	s/arm
Tyre size front	18	21	18	17
Tyre size rear	18	17	18	18
Dry weight (kg)	180	210	279	205